THE MOST IMPORTANT NON-SKALDIC
VERSE NOT INCLUDED IN
THE POETIC EDDA

BY
LEE M. HOLLANDER

Originally Published by
COLUMBIA UNIVERSITY PRESS
Morningside Heights: New York

* * * * * * *

Resurrected by
ABELA PUBLISHING
London
[2010]

Lee M. Hollander

Old Norse Poems

Typographical arrangement of this edition

© Abela Publishing 2010

This book may not be reproduced in its current format in any manner in any media, or transmitted by any means whatsoever, electronic, electrostatic, magnetic tape, or mechanical (including photocopy, file or video recording, internet web sites, blogs, wikis, or any other information storage and retrieval system) except as permitted by law without the prior written permission of the publisher.

Abela Publishing,
London
United Kingdom
2010

ISBN-13: 978-1-907256-50-9

email: Books@AbelaPublishing.com

www.AbelaPublishing.com/norsepoems.html

Old Norse Poems

Acknowledgments

Acknowledgments are due to the American-Scandinavian Foundation for permission to reprint—in a slightly different form—the translation of the *Biarkamól* and *The Oath of Truce*, which appeared in Axel Olrik's *The Heroic Legends of Denmark* and the *American-Scandinavian Review*.

****

Abela Publishing acknowledges the work that

Lee M. Hollander

did in publishing

Old Norse Poems

in a time well before any electronic media was in use.

****

Lee M. Hollander

Old Norse Poems

Contents

- Title Page i
- Acknowledgments iii
- Introduction 1
- Note 9
- The Old Lay of Biarki [Biarkamól hin Fornu] 11
- The Lay of Ingiald 29
- The Lay of Víkar [Víkarsbálkr] 39
- Hiálmar's Death Song 53
- The Lay of Hervor [Hervararkvitra] 59
- The Lay of Hloth and Angantýr [or The Battle of the Huns] 71
- The Lay of Innstein 91

  aka The Treachery of Ásmund

HILDIBRAND'S DEATH SONG 101

THE LAY OF HAROLD [HARALDSKVÆTHI OR

HRAFNSMÓL] 109

THE LAY OF ERIC [EIRÍKSMOL] 123

THE LAY OF HÁKON [HÁKONARMÓL] 129

THE SONG OF THE VALKYRIES [DARRA

THARLIOTH] 141

THE CURSE OF BUSLA [BUSLUBŒN] 149

THE OATH OF TRUCE [TRYGGTHAMÓL] 157

THE RIDDLES OF KING HEITHREK

[HEITHREKSGÁTUR] 165

THE SUN SONG [SÓLARLIÓTH] 197

Old Norse Poems

Old Norse Poems

INTRODUCTION

The group of poems here offered comprises practically all the more considerable (non-Skaldic) verse material not in the Edda. It shows, even better than that remarkable collection, of which it is intended to be the supplement, the wealth of independent poetic inventions and forms that flourished in the Scandinavian North before and immediately after the introduction of Christianity, especially when we bear in mind that much is irretrievably lost.

As to contents these poems, with respect to the first group of nine, range from the genuinely "heroic," realistic, dialogic-dramatic, earlier lays (such as the *Biarkamól*) to the more "romantic," legendary, monologic-elegiac, retrospective, *later* lays (like *Hiálmar's Death Song*); though the lines of demarcation are by no means sharp and, in fact, nearly every poem represents an individual combination of these traits. A very different type of lay is seen in the three contemporary encomiastic poems which celebrate the life and deeds of (historic) rulers of Norway — the only non-Skaldic efforts of this *genre* so exceedingly numerous in Old Norse literature. There is no common denominator for the four poems at the end of the volume, except possibly their arch-heathen character. As a finale the *Song of the Sun* marks the transition to Christian spheres of thought.

Common to all of this material, however, is its unliterary, that is, unbookish, character which is in marked contrast to virtually all of Anglo-Saxon epic literature, influenced as it is, to a greater or lesser degree, by Christian or classical models. That is to say, we deal here with the genuinely native expression of the North.

In particular, the "heroic" lays—figuring prominently also in the Edda, but occurring only sparsely in Anglo-Saxon and Old High German literature—are the concentrated expression of the ethos of Germanic antiquity, its poetry. The spirit which animates and dominates it is that of warfare under the leadership of men of heroic stature, in an age when the warlike nature p. xii of the Germanic race received an additional impulsion, viz., in that vast spectacle which we call the migration of nations; when through causes unknown to us and on a scale nowhere else recorded in history, many great and numerous peoples of Europe and Asia were set in motion and for the space of centuries wandered about in search of new homes; when the fortunes of war made swift kaleidoscopic changes in the map, and nations rose and fell overnight.

In such an age the purpose of song is not to beguile the time but to give to listeners a heightened sense of reality, of the verities of life lived nobly; to rouse emulation through a recital of the great deeds, the tragic fate, of the ancestors. Small wonder that the watchwords of life lived dangerously—of the maintenance of honor, even in defeat and death, through courage, energetic activity, generosity, loyalty to king, clan, friend—are dwelt upon to the exclusion of the gentler virtues of a settled life; and natural, that in this song there are recurrent patterns of action, such as the motives of revenge or lust for gold and power; that there are types, such as the guileless hero-king, the old wily despot, the stern grizzled warrior, rather than individuals; that the scenes are largely restricted to banquet hall and battle field. As a result, inevitably, a feeling of harsh and insistent monotony will be the first impression on readers of this literature, until greater familiarity with it will allow us, here too, to distinguish the individual in the type.

Turning to the technique employed in this literature, it will be noted that practically all is direct speech, monologue or dialogue, with hardly any narrative of action or description of scene or explanation of motive. As in the ballad of later times, all this is implied and suggested, frequently in a masterly fashion. To be sure, the whole art practice is addressed to an audience perfectly acquainted with the "story" (much as in our times a bygone generation was with biblical scenes) and to whom, therefore, the expression of the feelings alone was important. Often there is but one scene, dramatically tense, in which the quintessence of a life discharges itself in a sudden flash.

The vehicle for Old Germanic poetry is the alliterative verse, which in Old Norse poetic monuments is gathered into various stanzaic aggregates. Basic for it is the "short-line" of two stresses and an indeterminate number of unstressed syllables. Two such "short-lines," linked by alliteration—initial consonant riming with identical initial consonant, initial vowel with any initial vowel (note well, of stressed syllables only)—form a "long-line." Four of these, again, make up a stanza, which is called *fornyrthislag*, "old-lore meter" (as in *Hiálmar's Death Song*), if the number of unstressed syllables in each "short-line" is restricted, and *málaháttr*, "speech meter" (as in stanzas 3-8 of *Hákonarmól*), if the number of unstressed syllables is expanded.[1] The measure called *lióthaháttr*, "chant meter" (as in *Sólarlióth*) is peculiar in that each distich is formed by a "long-line" followed by a "full-line" with (generally) three stresses[2] and alliterating in itself. It is the (not invariable) rule that the alliteration in the second (even) "short-line" falls on the first stress only, whereas the first (odd) "short-line" may have two alliterative syllables.

With respect to the stress it is important to remember that there is no modern regularity, whether of its position in the line or of its alternating with unstressed syllable(s). Of the six mutations possible with a minimum of two accented and two unaccented syllables within a "short-line," only one is not permitted, viz., x x x´ x´. All others occur, viz., x´ x x´ x — x´ x´ x x — x x´ x´ x — x´ x x x´ — x x´ x x´ — [3] and will be found in this version.[4]

With slight exceptions, the poems here dealt with belong to Eddic art practice, which differs from Skaldic poetry in several p. xiv respects. Formally, Eddic verse occurs in the relatively simple meters outlined above; stylistically, it is for the most part in direct speech and uses few and relatively simple kennings. (A kenning is a figure of speech in which a person or thing is described or named by somebody or something else; in other words, it is a condensed simile. Thus, we may call a football player a "knight of the grid," and a Norwegian, a "son of the Vikings." In similar fashion, in the old poems, e.g., "battle" is called "Hild's (a valkyrie's) play" or "the meeting of swords," etc., and Óthin, "Sleipnir's rider" or "Frigg's husband," etc.). Skaldic poetry, on the other hand, is characterized, chiefly, by an exorbitant use of frequent and complicated kennings (cf. the purely Skaldic stanzas 6-8 of *Hákonarmól*). Also, the meters are generally more intricate, and there is scarcely ever direct speech.

The principal thing to keep in mind when reading Old Germanic verse is that, in consonance with the dramatic-passionate contents, the stress is dynamic, emphasizes content. Or, as it is better stated negatively: no stress, and therefore no alliteration, may fall on elements without an important increment of meaning. Obviously then, as we should not be misled, either, by our modern insistence on regularity of stress and equal length of lines, this verse is utterly alien to our ears. Then why translate into it, rather than into some more familiar form, or else why not resign oneself to prose? Because, I contend, no other verse form will approximate the feel of Old Germanic poetry: translation into any other form, however palatable in itself, radically fails in that respect. Hence, if it is worth while to become acquainted with Old Germanic poetry, it would seem worth while also to undergo the effort of reading the verse form in which it was given expression.

Similarly with the language. For heightened impressiveness and elevation, poets have always drawn on the hoarded treasure of their speech, paying with doubloons and ducats and pieces of eight, rather than with the current and trivial coin of the realm. So did the men who indited these lays. Hence I make p. xv no apology for occasional archaisms in my endeavor to recreate them on the speech level of the original. In this as in following the old metrical scheme I have preferred a true, rather than a smooth, rendering.

As readers I have had in mind, while preparing the introducions and the notes, especially the fairly numerous class of those interested in Anglo-Saxon literature, and the specialists in Old Norse not at all, and have therefore avoided dwelling on moot points. While of course leaning on the explorations of predecessors, I have generally sailed my own course—between reefs innumerable—with only occasional reference to the tracks of others.[5] Nevertheless I am afraid that in the notes I have erred both in giving too little and too much. On the one hand the whole world and *Weltanschauung* of the ancient North clamored for elucidation; on the other, as I well know, a plethora of notes is a weariness unto the flesh, besides interfering with the pleasure of reading

THE MOST IMPORTANT NON-SKALDIC
VERSE NOT INCLUDED IN
THE POETIC EDDA

Lee M. Hollander

ote

Pronunciation. — The acute accent over vowels signifies length. They are to be voiced in the Continental fashion, as in German or Italian. *G* is always hard, *s*, always surd. Word accent is invariably on the first syllable. The diphthongs ia, io, ill are rising.

Eddic Poems. — References to the Eddic poems are to the author's translation, *The Poetic Edda* (University of Texas Press, 1928).

Footnotes

1 A few examples of *kvithuháttr,* in which the odd lines have three, the even four, syllables, are found in the *Lay of Víkar*.

2 The efforts, notably of Heusler, to show that this line is but an expanded two-stress line, fail to convince me and, in fact, seem contradicted by the evidence. Cf. *The Journal of English and Germanic Philology,* 1931, pp. 475 f.

3 Adherence to these "Sievers Types" is not a matter of credulity on my part, as some of the critics of my Edda translation seem to imply, but of simple observation of the rhythmic facts.

4 The question of long or short syllable need not concern the reader of the translation.

5 The originals (nearly all) are most easily accessible in Heusler-Ranisch, *Eddica Minora,* and (all) in F. Jónsson's *Den Norsk-Islandske Skjaldedigtning*.

Lee M. Hollander

Old Norse Poems

The Old Lay of Biarki
[Biarkamól hin fornu]

IN A famous passage of his great book on the *History of the Norwegian Kings* (*Heimskringla*), Snorri relates how, early at morn, before the fatal battle of Stiklastad (1030), King Ólaf the Saint asked his skald (Thórmóth Kólbrunarskálld) to intone a song; whereupon he recited the *Old Biarkamól* (*Biarkamól hin fornu*) so that all the army could hear it, and all were pleased; and the men called the lay the *Exhortation of the Housecarls*[1] (*Húskarla hvot*). In the *Legendary Saga of Ólaf* we are told, furthermore, that when the king asked Thórmóth what boon he desired, that loyal heart asked for naught better than to be allowed to go before his king in battle, and that it might be granted to him not to survive his lord. "This answer is in the very spirit of the Biarkamól;"[2] as was the poem singularly well chosen, from out of the many Thórmóth no doubt knew, to fit the occasion, for it is a high song of devotion unto death—and everyone felt the king's to be a Lost Cause.

Unfortunately, only inconsiderable fragments have come down to us of this proud lay, though once it was known all over the North. For a conception of the whole poem we are now dependent on Saxo's spirited, but very free and wordy, translation into Latin hexameters,[3] and on the prolix and novelistic account of the late *Hrólfs saga kraka*. Taking these as his basis, aided by a strong poetic imagination, and with a profound knowledge of Old Norse poetry as a corrective, the Danish scholar, Axel Olrik, essayed to reconstruct the lay in its original form. As to the success of this difficult piece of restoration, one may question a detail, here and there, and yet agree that it is in the main true to the type, and rejoice in the successful restoration of a noble poem. For its meter Olrik chose the *málaháttr,* irregularly varying with *fornyrthislag,* which is seen in the few rests preserved. As to structure the poem consists of three long and chiefly lyrical parts of about equal size, separated from one another by brief dramatic interludes. In this decided preponderance of lyric over dramatic elements, as also in the leisurely breadth of the lyric passages, the lay reminds one of the Anglo-Saxon epics rather than of the poems of the Edda with their firmer structure and more energetic movement— whether now this be due to Danish origin or to the early date of the Icelandic lay used by Saxo. This is estimated by Olrik to be from about 900; but other scholars incline to a much later date (ca. 1200).

Putting together the accounts of Saxo and of the saga, the action is as follows: The great hero-king Hrólf kraki,[5] the son of Helgi (and nephew of Hróar), is assailed in his hall at Leire during the night by his vassal Hiorvarth, the ruler of the Gauts, who is incited to this treachery by his wife Skuld, Hrólf's own sister (or daughter). Hialti, a youthful champion in Hrólf's *hird,* arouses the inmates, and with taunting speeches exhorts them to fight and die for their generous lord, rallying them again and again. After a bitter struggle, Hiorvarth bursts through the castle gate, Hrólf falls, but his warriors continue to fight. The castle is fired, it seems by Hrólf's own men. Meanwhile, Biarki, his greatest champion, who has risen from poverty and finally married Hrólf's sister Hrút, lies in the hall in profound sleep, superinduced by Skuld's magic. He wakes at Hialti's third call and plunges into battle. But it is too late. Biarki sinks at his beloved chieftain's head, Hialti at his feet. When the battle dies down the mortally wounded Biarki is found by Hrút and made to see Óthin riding over the battle field. Dying, he defies him.[6]

The king remains throughout in the background, yet is the invisible center, worthy of the loyalty unto death of such warriors. They but reflect his glory—Biarki, towering up over the rest of them, the stern warrior, unyielding in death and defying even the king of the gods; beside him, brisk and steadfast, Hialti, his younger companion at arms, whose ringing alarums are thrice repeated, thanks to the happy retarding device of Biarki's magic sleep. Sharp lights fall even on the lesser characters, living and dead—on wicked Skuld, "by evil norns for ill created," and her husband Hiorvarth, swayed by her "to his kin to be false, his king to betray"; on the fierce warrlor Agnar who "laughs toward death"; on wretched King Hrœrek and gold-greedy King Athisl. Scelles of the present and the past flit by Hialti's and Biarki's inner vision, in their supreme hour—the glorious and deed-filled life of the housecarls in field and in banquet hall, under the eyes of the hero-king. Through their speeches we sense the hurly-burly, and feel the progress, of the battle. We learn of all the noble qualities which the upstanding, manly warrior-life of old allowed to unfold, and above all we appreciate that there may be glory in defeat.

Old Norse Poems

HIALTI

1. "Awake, arise, rally, friends!
   All ye foremost athelings of Hrólf!
   Awake not to wine nor to your wives' converse,
   but rather to Gondul's[7] game of war."

BIARKI

2. "Bring a fardel of fagots to kindle the fire!
   Brush thou the hearth and blow in the embers!
   Let the kindling crackle to kindle the logs:
   'tis winsome, with warm hand to welcome friends."[8]

   (drowsily responds, calling out to a thrall:)

(He relapses into sleep; but Hialti exhorts the housecarls and plunges into battle with his king:)

HIALTI

3 "Our great-hearted king gave to his housecarls
rings, helms, short-swords, and shining mail-coats;
his gifts in peace must be gained in war;
in war is proved what was pledged over ale.[9]

4 "The ruler of Danes chose him the doughty;
courage is known when the craven flee;
in the tumult of battle he needs trusty fighters:
conquest follows king who may count on his men.

5 "Hold firm your hilts, ye chosen housecarls,
shield flung on shoulder, to show ye are men;
breast open 'gainst breast offer we to our foemen:
beak against beak, so shall battle the eagles.

6 "Foremost among fighters bold Hiorvarth[10] fares,
glorying in swordplay, in gold-helm dight;
after him are marching martial hosts of Gauts,
with ring-laid[11] helms and rattling spears.

Old Norse Poems

7 "Skuld him egged on, the Skioldung[12] queen,
to his kin to be false, his king to betray;
raving she is and bereft of reason,
by evil norns for ill created."

(The tide of battle turns against Hrólf and he falls. Hialti continues:)

8 "Now their last cup for kingsmen is poured,
after his liege-lord shall no one live
but he show him fearful and shrink from blows,
or be too listless his lord to avenge.

9 "Our byrnies are slit and sundered our limbs;
blows of the bill have broken the king's shield;
wide gapes the gate, and the gallant flee,
the baleful battle-axe gnaws men's brows.

10 "Lift thou now, Hrút, thy light-haired brow,
leave thy bower, for battle is nigh.

* * *

the towers are tumbling, the castle-gates tremble."

(Hialti and his men fire the castle. They discover Biarki in profound sleep:)

HIALTI

11 "Bidest thou yet, Biarki? Do sleep-runes[13] bind thee?
Come forth now with me ere thee fire assail!
We fend off our foes as we do bears—with firebrands:[14]
the castle crumbles, the king's hall flames."

(As Biarki still tarries, Hialti once more rallies his warriors:)

HIALTI

12 "Let us rally our ranks as Hrólf us taught,
the hero who hewed down the ring-hoarder.
Wretched was Hrœrek though he riches owned:
but gold he gathered, not gallant men.

13 "Hrólf harried on Hrœrek. He ransom offered—
before the gates disgorged his purse its gold:
he strewed before stronghold stores of treasure.[15]
Then was lavished on foe what on friends was saved.

Old Norse Poems

14 "Though our liege him slew: he allotted the hoard
among faithful followers, refused it himself.
Nothing him gladdened but he gave it to them:
to award it to warriors naught was too welcome.

15 "The most large-hearted lord lifeless has sunk;
lost is the life men will longest remember:
he ran to the sword-play as river toward sea,
fared against foe like the fleet-footed stag.

16 "A burn of blood from the battle-field flows,
as Hjorvarth arnong hosts Hild's-play[16] speedeth.
But the sword-giver smiles in his sleep of death,
as at bountiful banquet he beakers emptied.

17 "Fróthi's kinsman[17] on the Fýri Plains
his gold rings sowed, glad in his mind;
him we joyfully follow on his journey to Hel,
manly of speech and firm of mettle.

18 "Blows of our brands shall back our faith,
the glory of great deeds never is forgotten.
Latched and locked the hall still is right.
A third time, Biarki, I bid thee come forth!"

BIARKI

19 "Eagerly doest thou, Hialti, egg on Hrólf's kinsman;[18]
but to vaunting words fit valiant deeds.
Bide thou whilst Biarki his byrnie fastens;
little he lists to be burned alive.

20 "On an isle was I born, barren and little;
twelve demesnes gave me Hrólf to master,
realms to rule, and ruddy gold, too—
his sister to wife; here's worth to requite.
   (He plunges into battle:)

21 "Shields on your shoulders, if ye shun not death!
Only the craven covers him now.
Bare your breasts! Your bucklers fling down![19]
Gold-weighted arm the glaive best wields.[20]

Old Norse Poems

22 "With my steel erst I struck the wild stag[21] in battle,
with my short-sword slew him which Snirtir is named.
Hero's name got I when its hilt I gripped—
when Agnar Ingialdsson's life I ended.

23 "'Gainst my head he hewed, but Hœking[22] broke,
on Biarki's brow his blade was shattered.
Then raised I Snirtir, through his ribs thrust him,
his right hand and right leg I lopped with one blow.

24 "Never was there, I ween, a more warlike hero
than when, sword-hewn, sank the son of Ingiald:
lifeless he lay and laughed toward death;
to Valhall's gates he gleefully hied him.

25 "To his heart I hewed the hero but now,
young in years but unyielding in spirit;
through his buckler I battered, naught booted him his hauberk:
my Snirtir but seldom slackens its blow.

21

26 "Guard you now, ye gallant Gautish chieftains!
Athelings only enter this battle!

. . .
. . .

27 "His loved son now loses many a lord;
but for barons, not bondmen Hel's bars will be lowered.
More closely comes the clash of battle,
three blows I get for one I give.

28 "Alone in the strife I stand amongst the slain.
A bulwark I build me of fallen bodies.
Where is now he who whetted me before,
and tempted me sore, as though twelve lives he had?"

HIALTI

29 "Few are the followers, but far I am not.
Strong is now need of stout-hearted men;
battered is my buckler, broken and shattered—
yourself may see it: sight goes before hearsay.
Doest battle now, Biarki, as thou didedst before?"

BIARKI

30 "Thy spiteful speech   spurs me no longer:
not I am the cause   that tardy I came.
Now a Swedish sword   sorely has struck me;
through my war-weeds it went   as though water it cleft."

(Biarki's wife Hrút has found her mortally wounded husband on the battle field, where the conflict is now dying down.)

31 "But where is Óthin,   the one-eyed grey-beard?
Say now, Hrút, swiftly: Seest thou him nowhere?"

HRÚT

32 "Lower thy eye   and look through my arm,[23]
sign then thy view   with victory-runes:
unscathed shalt thou, Biarki,   then scan with thy glance
and fasten thy eyes   on the father of victory."[24]

BIARKI

33 "Could I fasten my eyes on Frigg's husband[24] now,
the swift shield-swinger and Sleipnir's rider,
his life would lose the war-god at Leire[25]—
blood for blood then would Biarki crave.

34 "Here by my chieftain's head I shall sink now,
thou[26] by his feet shalt find thee a rest.
Booty-seekers on battle field shall bear me out:
the great-souled king's gifts even the dead forget not.

35 "Soon greedy eagles will gorge on our bodies,
ramping ravens will rend our limbs.
To high-minded, hardy hero it is seeming
dying to dwell by his king rich in deeds."

Old Norse Poems

Footnotes

1 The housecarls of the Scandinavian kings correspond to the *hird* of the Anglo-Saxons. They formed the bodyguard of select warriors.

2 Axel Olrik, *The Heroic Legends of Denmark* (English trans., 1916) p. 169.

3 *Gesta Danorum,* book II.

4 Among other things, it may be doubted whether the lay was a pure dialogue poem and not, as were the oldest lays, interspersed with narrative.

5 The matter of Hrólf's rise, but not his fall, is briefly alluded to in various passages of *Bēowulf*.

6 For a detailed and searching analysis the reader is referred to Olrik's work, pp. 202 f.

7 (Or Hild), one of the Valkyries. In Snorri's account, the beginning is as follows:

> The day has come, claps the cock his wings:
> 'tis time for thralls to go to their tasks.
> Awake, ye friends, be aye awake,
> all ye best men of Athil's board.

Hár the hard-gripping, Hrólf the bowman,
men of noble race who never flee;
I wake you not to wine nor to women's converse,
but rather to the hard game of Hild.

But for reasons, fully discussed by Olrik, these stanzas cannot have been the beginning of the *Old Biarkamól*.

8 It is uncertain whether he thinks guests are coming or ironically bids the enemies welcome with fire (cf. stanza 11).

9 Almost all the phrases in this stanza, and many others in the following exhortation, recur verbally in Wīglāf's exhortation of Bēowulf's men to support him against the dragon (*Bēowulf*, 11, 2663-2660); and much occurs of the same import in the *Battle of Maldon*.

10 Equivalent to Anglo-Saxon *Heoroweard*. Other names, in the lay, have the following Anglo-Saxon equivalents: *Helgi, Hālga; Hróar, Hrōthgār; Hrólf, Hrōthulf;* the Gauts *(Gautar), Gēatas; Hrærek, Hrēthrīk; Ingiald, Ingeld; Athils, Ēadgils.*

11 Helmets adorned with chains of rings.

12 *Skioldungs* (Anglo-Saxon, *Scyldingas*), the royal race of Denmark, whose progenitor is *Skiǫld* (Anglo-Saxon, *Scyld*).

13 Cf. the magic runes fettering Sigrdrífa, *Sigrdrífumǫl*, Prose after stanza 4.

14 In Saxo: *igne ursos arcere licet.* Possibly, an allusion to Biarki's name, which is a "short-name" for a name compounded with -*bjǫrn,* "bear." He has by some scholars been identified with Bēowulf.

15 In order to purchase peace.

16 One of the valkyries; hence, "Hild's-play," a kenning for "battle."

17 *I.e.,* Hrólf. — The allusion is to an expedition of Hrólf to King Athils of Sweden. When treacherously pursued by Athils on the Fýri Plains (*i.e.,* the region of Upsala) Hrólf stopped him by scattering gold rings which Athils and his men greedily picked up.

18 Biarki himself.

19 Cf. *Hákonarmól,* stanza 4.

20 *I.e.,* the golden arm-ring, by reminding warriors of the generosity of their lord, will cause them to fight more spiritedly.

21 A kenning, it seems, for "warrior."

22 Agnar's sword. Its name signifies "the sword owned by Hók."

23 One who possesses second-sight can make others see what he sees by letting them look through his bended arm supported on his hip. The victory-runes are the same, apparently, as those referred to in *Sigrdrífumól,* stanza 7.

24 Óthin, who has been aiding the enemy and is now collecting the dead warriors for Valholl. He rides the eight-footed steed Sleipnir. Cf. *Grímnismól,* stanza 44.

25 Old Norse *Hleithrar,* the capital of the Danish kingdom in prehistoric times.

26 Hialti.

Old Norse Poems

The Lay of Ingiald

IN THE sixth book of Saxo Grammaticus's *Gesta Danorum* there are embedded, in the narrative of the Danish hero, Starkath's, life and deeds, two extensive poems, the *Lay of Ingiald* and *Starkath's Death Song;* and a third lay, somewhat related to the Icelandic *Víkarsbálk*, is to be inferred from Saxo's prose narrative. That there were current lays about Starkath, not only in Scandinavia, but also in Anglo-Saxon England, brought thither from the old home, and that they were in favor, is amply evident from that reproachful passage in one of Alcuin's letters:[1] "Quid enim Hinieldus cum Christo? Angusta est domus; utrosque tenere non poterit" — What hath Ingiald to do with Christ? Small is the house, it will not hold both — even if we did not have the well-known Ingeld episode of *Bēowulf* (2024-2069).

Like the *Biarkamól,* and likewise Danish in origin, the *Lay of Ingiald* is an "exhortation" — even more narrowly so — not to loyal devotion unto death in the king's cause, but addressed to the son of the slain father, to bestir himself to revenge. Both the situation and the reaction to it are typical of the Germanic North in pre-Christian times.

According to the oldest, and no doubt most original, account as found in *Bēowulf,* the matter is as follows: In a great battle with the Heathobards,[2] their king, Frōda, was slain. In order to effect a reconciliation between the two hostile nations, the Danish king, Hrōthgār, gave his daughter, Frēawaru, in marriage to Ingeld, the son of Frōda; but at the marriage feast—it seems, in the royal hall of the Heathobards—a young warrior, stung to the quick by the repeated eggings on of an old warrior, slays one of the Danish company, in order to avenge his father. Ingeld's love of the Danish princess "cools" (*i.e.*, he puts her away), the feud breaks out again which according to *Wīdsīth*, ends with the disastrous defeat of the Heathobards before Heorot, the royal hall of the Danes.

This matter is significantly changed, and condensed to far greater dramatic effect, in the Old Danish lay. There, the injured party are the Danes, the ignominious peace and marriage lies in the past. Starkath, the stern old warrior and companion in arms of Fróthi, arrives incognito in Leire, where a sumptuous banquet is being given by Ingiald to his brothers-in-law (here called the sons of Sverting), and arouses him by bitter denunciation of his supineness to slay them and put away their sister, his wife. To the rôle of the formidable hereditary enemies of the land have succeeded the Germans[3]—as well they might under the powerful and aggressive (Saxon) Ottones, who finally compelled the Danes to accept their overlordship and Christianity. The lay has gained, furthermore, by the fierce denunciation of the new and hated Southron ways and by concentrating this invective on Ingiald; who avenges himself on the spot.

Starkath's own personality is kept in the background, though he is unmistakably felt to be *the* representative of the older and better ideals of the Viking Age. Since this age, to which the lay harks back with such approbation, had come to an end in the ninth century, after the conquest and settlement of the western and northern Atlantic littoral; since the poem is still thoroughly heathen in spirit; and since the fear and hatred of the Saxon and his ways could have arisen only after the accession of the Saxon emperors, it is safe to conclude that the lay was composed during the tenth century.

As for its contents, we are altogether dependent on Saxo's prolix and highly rhetorical Latin version—in Sapphic stanzas and hexameters.[4] From these, Olrik by judicious reduction brought out the lay approximately as it may have come to the knowledge of Saxo. The version here offered leans on Olrik's, but is shorter by nine stanzas through the elimination of some fulsome details improbable in an old lay and, especially, the omission of the weak ending which in Olrik's version mars the fine climax of exultation over the revenge accomplished, which Starkath calls on Óthin to witness.

1 "Go from the grey-beard! No longer make game of me,
   ye deedless swains in the Danish court!
   No outcast is the old man before you:
   oft hoary hair hideth a hardy mind.

2 "I formerly followed Fróthi for years,
   sate in the high-seat,5 and was served before others;
   but now I sit nameless and unknown in the hall,
   I like a fish at ebb-tide finding a waterhole.

3 "I formerly sate on soft cushions;
   now in a corner I sit, crowded by every one.
   Fain out of doors would they drive the grey-beard
   but wall and wainscot gave welcome foothold.

4 "The courtiers laugh at me who come from afar off,
   no one gets up to greet me or to cheer the guest!
   What be the ways now in the hall of the Skioldungs?
   I should like to learn Leire's6 new breeding.

Old Norse Poems

5 "Thinkest thou, Ingjald, as at ease thou sittest,
to avenge Fróthi, thy father, on his banesmen?
Or are you pleased, rather to fill your paunch
than to make stern war on the murderers of your father?

6 "That feared I, when farewell to the folkwarder I said,
that slain by the sword he soon would lie.
From Fróthi afar the folklands I roamed
when I learned that our liege had been laid low by Saxons.

7 "Had *that* time I been with the thane's shield-bearers,
then not deedless had I seen my dear lord's fall:
my sword had then smitten the Saxon traitors,
or else had I fallen by Fróthi's side.

8 "Now on wilding ways I wended from Sweden,
hoping to find Fróthi's heir-taker—
and find a feaster but for food hankering,
and instead of a king, a coward and wanton.

33

9 "But sooth did say the Swedish king—7
that 'deedless scions follow doughty father.'
Shall strangers steal the stores of your father?
Shall his red-gold rings fall in robbers' hands?"

(Then the queen, frightened, and wishing to appease the terrible old man, undid her golden fillet and handed it to him; but Starkath hurled it back at her scornfully and said:)

10 "Away from the warrior with your woman's finery!
About your own brow bind your fillet,
or else your husband's, who will highly prize it,
fingering for food steaked fowls' inwards.

11 "Evil art, thou, Ingiald's mistress!
Saxland's ways soft to Sealand thou broughtest!
In the king's kitchen cook they now tidbits,
such as war-workers ne'er would have eaten.

12 "But on board, bloody, the meat of beeves[8]
was laid for strong men as they right the battlefield.
In their frosted beards oft bit the rowers,
nor slaked their thirst with sweet milk for babies.

Old Norse Poems

13   "Athelings eleven, all told, were there
     with Haki,[9] when we rode the horse-of-the-sea.[10]
     Beigath and Belgi at board with us sate;
     seldom on sea fared swains more hardy.

14   "With smoked salt meat we sated our hunger,
     and slaked our thirst with swallows of ale;
     nor was honeyed mead ever Haki's delight,
     nor soft bread, either, when at sea he fared.

15   "But weregild no one e'er would have taken,
     or by payment of pence in his purse borne his father;[11]
     nor was ever heard that the heir of his father
     sate at festive board with his father's banesmen.

16   "So, when in the hall great heroes are spoken of,
     and skalds are chanting the champions' great deeds,
     then in shame I hide under hood my glances,
     for Fróthi's first-born showed but faint-heartedness.

17 "Why so sternly, Ingiald, starest thou at me?
Never saw the sneering Saxons such glances!
Thou who never didst win other warfare
than cutting down bread and killing puddings.

18 "A cruel fate has befallen Fróthi's kinsmen
when the king was given such a coward as heir:
no greater worth hast thou than a hunted goat,
or than sheep in shambles shrinking in terror.

19 "Shall Sverting's[12] seed hold sway over Denmark,
Seated at Leire with Saxon warriors,
on thy lap whilst thou fondlest the linen-clad woman,
the fair-haired daughter of thy father's banesman.

(Roused by these words, Ingiald leapt up and drew his sword on Sverting's sons who sat in the high-seat with him.)

20 "Rail now, Ingiald! Thou art awakened!
No more wavering weakness, thou warriors' leader,
but slay with the sword all of Sverting's kinsmen!
Alike be their death as alike was their deed!

21 "Let thralls drag then the dead from the high-seat,
cart away the killed ones from the king's mead-hall,
toss the dead out-of-doors— nor dig graves for them—
to feed on the heath foxes and ravens.

22 "Still further shalt, Ingjald, if foresight thou hast,
put away the woman wily and evil
The she-wolf's whelps will take after *her:*
beware of the wolf though weak he be now.

23 "Behold now, Hrauthi,[13] thou who whettest to strife,
that full vengeance for Fróthi is taken:
the seven sons of Sverting by sword are laid low,
his false friends now are felled by Ingjald.

24 "Though hoary my hair that hope never left me
that Fróthi's first-born would not flinch in trial;
as only heir shall Ingjald rule here
over the lands of the Danes and Leire's high-seat."

Footnotes

1 A.D. 797.

2 This warlike tribe was located south of Denmark, north of the lower Elbe.

3 Or "Saxons" as they are called, from the nearest German tribe.

4 The metre of the original is assumed to have been *málaháttr*.

5 The raised seat of honor in the middle of the hall. The seats for servants and hangers-on were at the gable-end, near the door.

6 Cf. *Biarkamól,* note 25.

7 With whom Starkath had dwelt during his absence.

8 Cf. the *Second Lay of Helgi,* stanzas 8, 9.

9 Typical name for a viking.

10 Kenning for "ship."

11 To "carry one's kinsman in one's purse" was a current expression of utmost contumely for enriching one's self by accepting weregild, instead of avenging him.

12 The king of the Saxons.

13 "The Destroyer;" which seems to be a name of Óthin, the inciter to warfare.

Old Norse Poems

The Lay of Víkar
[VÍKARSBÁLKR]

THIS FINE but difficult retrospective monologue is unique in Old Germanic literature; not so much in manner as in matter. Its hero is, to be sure, the Danish national champion, Starkath, celebrated in song and story (though this lay is the only extant poetic treatment of the theme in the original language); but in this episode he has undergone a change to the sinister and demonic. The stern warrior and unbending protagonist of the olden simplicity of morals and customs, such as he appears in the *Lay of Ingiald* and elsewhere, has here become an uncouth half-troll of superhuman strength and somewhat dubious, Ahasveric nature. But the lay bespeaks an unexpected sympathy for this composite character of mixed heroism and baseness. His crime, the most heinous, according to Old Germanic ethics, of treacherously slaying his leader and foster brother to whom he is, moreover, genuinely attached because he owes to him his awakening to the heroic life—this crime is not to be expiated by "repentance." To be sure, the accompanying story, both in the *Gautreks saga*, in which the lay is interwoven, and in Saxo seeks at least to motivate, and thus palliate, the deed by laying the blame on Óthin[1]—in all the Starkath lays he is the instigator to strife. But, of course, it is the troll nature that reveals itself finally, making him a "nithing."

As to the prose of the *Gautreks saga* and the similar story of Saxo,[2] it seems to occupy a middle ground in technique: it is not mainly supererogatory and explicatory stage direction, as in the oldest lays—say, the *Lays of Skirnir*, of *Volund*; nor a wordy setting for lays elaborating, and based on, themes taken from it—as, say, the *Lay of Hiálmar*; but has an independent value beside the lay, furnishing legendary facts which the lay may not even hint at, just as the lay in its turn is independent of the prose. Hence a full account is given below of the somewhat complicated story.

There is hardly a question about the Icelandic origin, say in the twelfth century, of this vigorous and pithy poem. The poor state of transmission necessitates a number of drastic emendations. *Fornyrthislag*, with a few *kvithuháttr* lines interspersed, is the meter employed.

As the *Hálf's saga* relates, in its first chapter, the sacrifice of Víkar to Óthin came about in the following manner: Beautiful Geirhild managed to be taken as wife by King Alrek of Horthaland[3] through Óthin's help, on condition that she should call on the god in all difficulties. King Alrek was married already to Signy, the daughter of another king. The two wives could not agree, and Alrek promised that he would retain as his queen her who brewed the best ale against his return. Signy called on Freya, and Geirhild on Óthin. He added his spittle for yeast and said that for his help he must have that which was between her and the vat. Her ale proved to be the best. Then said Alrek:

> "Beware, Geirhild! Good is this ale,
> if not any evil follow:
> on high gallows hanging I see
> thy son, Geirhild, given to Óthin.'"

That same year was born their son Víkar.

As to Starkath's origin and youth, we learn from the *Gautreks saga*, Chapter 3, that his grandfather, the giant Starkath, robbed a princess. Her father called for aid on Thór, inveterate enemy of the giant tribe, who slew Starkath and led her back to her father. She gave birth to Stórvirk—"a handsome man, though black of hair, larger and stronger than other men." He becomes right-hand man of King Harold of Agthir. In his turn, Stórvirk abducts Unni, Earl Freki's daughter. This deed is avenged in time by the earl's two sons, Fiori and Fýri. They burn Stórvirk and Unni in their hall, but the infant Starkath survives the fire and is adopted by King Harold. When three years old he is taken thence and fostered by an old man called Hrosshársgrani (*i.e.*, Óthin) at Ask,[4] where he grows to the age of twelve, uncouth and huge of strength, but unaware of his powers. Under the same fosterage, and as hostage, grew up also Víkar, the son (here) of the same King Harold who, meanwhile, was treacherously slain by a neighboring king, Herthióf. Víkar becomes a great leader and, joined by Starkath, whom he arouses to action, and eleven other young warriors, he avenges his father on Herthióf and wins back his kingdom. On all his various ensuing expeditions Starkath is his trusted friend and companion and distinguishes himself by deeds of valor.

One time, Víkar is held back with his fleet by contrary winds. They consult the oracle, which pronounces that Óthin must be appeased by the sacrifice of a man. The lot falls on King Víkar. That same night, Hrosshársgrani comes to Starkath and bids him follow him. They row to land. In a forest close at hand the gods are assembled, debating Starkath's fate. Óthin, his foster father and protector, bestows on him all manner of good things, among them, the gift of poetry and three lives; but Thór, Óthin's antagonist, who moreover hates Starkath by reason of his giant origin, adds a misfortune to each gift: in each life he is to commit some dastardly deed. Óthin, in return for his gifts, bids Starkath send him Víkar. He consents. On the morrow, Starkath proposes to the fleet to make a mock sacrifice of Víkar to Óthin. He induces the king to let him fasten about his neck the soft guts of a calf, which he attaches to a slender branch of a tree. Then Starkath touched him with a reed and said: "now I give thee to Óthin," and let go of the branch. But the branch lifted Víkar up quickly, the guts did their service, and the reed became a spear and pierced him.[5] Starkath is outlawed and flees to the Swedish court where the taunting of inferior men arouses the "speechless poet" to unburthen his heart in the following monologue.

1   "A boy was I when they burned in hall,
    with my father, the warrior host—
    not far outside the firth of Thruma.6

2   "Was Harold of Agthir's host overthrown—
    had his kinsmen bewrayed the ring-breaker,
    Fiori and Fýri, earl Freki's heirs.
    Were they Unni's brothers, my own mother's;

3   "the time Herthióf Harold betrayed,
    betrayed the king who trusted in him.
    He robbed of his life the liege of Agthir,
    and fetters fastened for his twain sons.

4   "Me three winters old thence did bring
    Hrosshársgrani8 to Northaland;
    at Ask gan I grow and strengthen,
    saw none of my sib for nine summers.

5   "Strength gat I mighty, grew stalwart my arms,
    and long my legs, loathly my head;
    as a gaby, dozing I gaping sate,
    listless and lazy, on lower bench.9

6   "Then Víkar wended, from watch-fire faring,[10]
    Herthióf's hostage, into the hall.
    He knew me again by name and bade me
    up to arise and answer him.

7   "With hands and fingers he fathomed me:
    were all my arms (much etin-like,)[11]
    to the wrists downward (rough and hairy,)[11]
    and my face bearded from brow to chin.

8   "Then Harold's heir[12] the host gathered:
    Sorkvir and Grettir and Hildigrím,
    Erp and Ulf, Án and Skúma,
    Hrói and Hrotti, which were Herbrand's sons,

9   "Stýr and Steinthór from Stath[13] in the North,
    gathered also old Gunnólf blesi.[14]
    Were then of us thirteen together:
    a hardier host will hardly be found.

10 "To Herthióf's hall we hied us then,
    shook its door-posts, broke down its gates,
    shattered its bars, brandished our swords
    where stood seventy stalwart warriors.[15]

45

11 "We vied with each other, Víkar to follow[16]
since first and foremost in the flock he stood;
we hewed helmets and the heads that bore them,
sundered byrnies and broke through shields.

12 "Was great glory granted to Víkar,
but Herthiof paid for his hateful deed:
some we wounded, and slew others;
not far was I stead[17] when fell the king.

13 "On the Vænir[18] wert not with Víkar then,
east in the land at early morn,
in the field when we fought with Sísar:[19]
were those doughty deeds of undying fame.

14 "With his sword did he sorely wound me—
sharp-edged was it— through my shield cleaving.
My helm he hewed from off my head,
my chin he cleft clean to the jawteeth.[20]

15 "And on one side with his sword he cut me—
mightier than I— the midriff above;
but through the other he thrust his spear,
the cold iron, within it stood.[21]

Old Norse Poems

16 "With my sword, Sísar's side I cut then
with bitter brand, his belly athwart.
So wrathfully I raised my sword
that all my strength I bestowed on it.

* * *[22]

17 "Much Welsh gold gave me Víkar—
the red-gold ring which on wrist I wear,
of three marks' weight;[23] I Thruma[24] gave him.
I followed the king fifteen summers.

18 "I followed the king whom foremost I knew:
my life did I like best then.
'T was ere we fared— did foul trolls drive us—
to Northaland: this happened last.

19 "The outcome this, that Thór gave me
a nithing's[25] name, unnumbered woes—

* * *

I was fated fell things to do.

20 "In high tree was I to hallow Víkar,
to give to the gods Geirthiof's[26] slayer.
Through his heart I thrust the thane with my spear:
of all my works most woeful this!

21 "On wilding ways I wandered thence,
    by the Horthar[27] hated, with heart rueful,
    bereft of rings and robbed of honor,
    leaderless, forlorn in mind.

22 "Now have I sought the Swedish lands,
    the Ynglings'[28] seat, Uppsala halls.
    A speechless poet,[29] the prince's sons
    did let me stay— as long I shall.

23 "They set me here brash[30] swains between,
    who scornfully scoff at the aged skald;
    gleefully girding, they make game of me,
    and lewdly laugh at the liege's poet.

24 "They ween they see on my own self
    the etin mark of eight arms,
    the time Hlórrithi[31] Hergrím's slayer[32]
    reft of his arms in the outmost North.

25 "The men laugh when looking at me—
    at my loathly mug and long snout,
    my wolf-grey hair and hanging arms,
    my scurvy neck and wrinkled skin."

Old Norse Poems

Footnotes

1 Cf. also the *Second Lay of Helgi,* 34: "of all evil is Óthin father." It is instructive to compare the Herakles of Euripides in this respect.

2 Who derives it from Norwegian sources.

3 The southwestern district of Norway, as Agthir (below) is the southernmost.

4 On the island of Fenhring, near the present city of Bergen. The implied hostility of these divinities, and Óthin's assumption, on an island, of the tutelage of his favorite in sinister arts, recall the story of Geirrœth in the prose of *Grímnismál*.

5 This story, told similarly by Saxo, is a reminiscence of the human sacrifices—by hanging and piercing with a spear—which belonged to the worship of Óthin, the "god of the hanged" (*Hávamál,* 139.) The circumstances of the sacrifice resemble closely that of the sacrifice of Iphigenia in Greek lore.

6 The present Tromö-sund, a sound between the island of Tromö and the mainland, near Arendal, on the southeast coast of Norway.

7 It appears that he joined forces with Freki, and fell upon both King Harold and Starkath's father. We are not told who Víkar's brother was.

8 "Man with a mustache of (or like) horse hair": Óthin, who is frequently pictured as a greybeard.

9 Where the strvants ate: Starkath as a youth grows up as the typical ashiepattle, huge of body, who conceals his wits (and his plans of revenge?) under the guise of a tongue-tied zany. Cf. Helgi in the *Lay of Helgi Hiorvarthsson*.

10 Herthióf had instituted beacon signals to warn of hostile raids, and Víkar was set over one of them.

11 Lines lacking in the original and supplied here by guess of the translator.

12 Víkar.

13 The promontory in the west of Norway.

14 "White-face."

15 The MSS add the following (later?) lines:

> "unafraid of the fray, before their king.
> Were there also all of the thralls,
> the working men and water-carriers."

16 In the original, "it was hard to follow," etc., a somewhat unusual thought.

17 Litotes: Starkath slays him.

18 Vænir is the great Swedish lake on whose frozen surface this, and other, battles were fought. The following is more particularly addressed to the king's man who had taunted Starkath.

[19] This redoubtable antagonist bears the name of the Russian Czar (from *Cisari,* Cæsar).

[20] The MSS add:

> "my right collar-bone he crushed with a blow."

The description of mortal and disfiguring wounds and of other blemishes is peculiar to the poem.

[21] The MSS add:

> "canst see on me the marks yet, healed."

[22] At this point, the original contains eight stanzas, inferior in value and quite evidently interpolated, dealing with further deeds of Víkar, but speaking of Starkath in the third person.

[23] A "mark" was eight ounces.

[24] Which island King Harold had given Starkath's father.

[25] "Base villain and coward"; a term difficult to render in English with one vocable. The stanza is defective, but evidently the happenings on the island to which Óthin took Starkath in the night are referred to. The broken style betrays the agitation of the speaker.

[26] Another king, Herthióf's brother, slain by Víkar.

27 The inhabitants of Horthaland.

28 The royal race of Sweden, descended from the god Yngvi-Frey.

29 The exact meaning of Old Norse *thulr* (here translated "poet") is not certain, especially in this passage. If the meaning generally attributed to it, and here followed, is correct, then we may surinise that the gift of poetry given Starkath by Óthin was denied utterance by Thór. The princes allow Starkath to remain silent, brooding over his treachery. For once, he bursts out — with self-accusation, not in repentance. And he means to relapse into silence, for a long time.

30 The "white-browed" of the original I take to refer to their immaturity, contrasted with Starkath's swart hairiness.

31 Thór.

32 The older Starkath.

Old Norse Poems

Hiálmar's Death Song

Like the *Víkarsbálk* and *Hildibrand's Death Song*, this essentially monologic lay belongs to a category which forms a masculine counterpart to the feminine retrospective poems of the Edda, such as *Helreith Brynhildar* and *Guthrúnarhvǫt*: at the point of death, or in the beyond, the speaker lets pass in review the events of his life. This conventional situation conditions a lyric-elegiac mood; which finds especially beautiful, if somewhat facile and not very original, expression in our poem. And inasmuch as there is stress laid on the melancholy "nevermore" of lovers beset by a tragic fate, rather than on deeds of valor, we may even speak of a quasi-Romanticism. Indeed, external reasons likewise point to thirteenth-century origin, when medieval influences made themselves felt in the upper levels of Northern society, and French romances and lais were being translated voluminously.

Two versions exist, both derived from one now lost—the one in a MS of the *Hervarar saga;* the other, both longer and better, in the *Orvar Odds saga,* which accordingly has been rendered here. However, the lay does not fit organically into the latter saga.

53

Piecing together the accounts in both sagas, the story of Hiálmar is as follows: Angantýr, a ferocious Viking chief, makes a Yuletide vow that he will wed beautiful Ingibiorg, the daughter of King Yngvi at Uppsala in Sweden, or else die. But when he appears there, the princess rejects him in favor of Hiálmar, right-hand man of the king, whom she loves. Thereupon Angantýr challenges Hiálmar to single combat, next summer, on the island of Samsey. There, Hiálmar and his companion at arms, the redoubtable Orvar Odd (or Sóti), encounter Angantýr and his eleven berserker brothers. Hiálmar slays Angantýr, notwithstanding the latter's invincible sword Tyrfing, but is mortally wounded himself. Orvar Odd (or Sóti), protected by a magic silk shirt, is the sole survivor.

Old Norse Poems

SÓTI said:

1. "What ails thee, Hjálmar? Thy hue is pale.
   Great wounds, I ween, do weary thee;
   thy helmet is hewn, thy hauberk eke:
   at an end is now, atheling, thy life!"

HJÁLMAR said:

2. "Wounds have I sixteen, is slit my byrnie,
   dim grows my sight, I see no longer:
   to my heart did hew, venom-hardened,
   Angantýr's sword slashing sharply.

3. "Shall fair ladies never learn that I,
   from blows me shielding, backward turned me;
   nor shall ever Ingibjorg taunt me,
   in Sigtúna sitting, that from sword-blows I fled.

4. "Unwilling nowise, from women's converse,
   from their sweet songs I with Soti fared,
   hastened to join the host to eastward,
   went the last time forth from friends so dear.

Lee M. Hollander

5 "Led me the white-browed liege's daughter
   to the outmost end of Agnafit.[2]
   Is borne out thus that back I would not
   wend from this war: so the wise maid said.

6 "From Ingibiorg— came ill-hap swiftly—
   I fared forth, then, on fated day:
   a lasting sorrow to the lady, this,
   since not e'er after each other we'll see.

7 "To have and to hold I had five manors;
   on that land to live misliked me, though.
   Now, robbed of life, I lie here, spent,
   by the sword wounded, on Sáms-isle's shore.

8 "Take with thee, Soti— my wish it is—
   my helm and hauberk to the hall of the king.
   Will it wring the heart of the ruler's daughter
   when shattered she sees what shielded my breast.

Old Norse Poems

9   "The red-gold ring from my right arm draw,
    to Ingibiorg bring it, in her bower sitting.
    Will yearn for me the young maiden,
    since not e'er after each other we'll see.

10 "I see sitting in Sigtúna hall
    the women who warned me of wending thence.
    Will not ever after ale nor warriors
    Hjálmar gladden here in this life.

11 "Quaff with the king the crowd of housecarls
    their ale gladly in Uppsala;
    doth the mead many men overcome,
    but me overmaster here many wounds.

12 "Flies from the South the famished raven,
    flieth with him the fallow eagle;
    on the flesh of the fallen I shall feed them no more:
    on my body both will batten now."

Footnotes

1 Between Uppsala and the present Stockholm.
2 This is a low flat point south of the present Stockholm.

Old Norse Poems

The Lay of Hervor
[Hervararkvitha]

SOME students have doubted whether this lay, which to them seems episodic, was composed and recited independently of the saga in which it occurs. They seem to forget that its substance is not merely Hervor conjuring up her father from the dead, and with her malisons compelling him to yield to her out of the grave the precious heirloom of the wondrous invincible sword buried with him: this action is only preparatory of the dire prophecy bound up with the ownership of Tyrfing, the sword which demands the life of a man, every time it is drawn, and "must be sheathed in warm blood." The fact that the prophecy of the total annihilation of her progeny, as stated here, does not square with the account of the saga may mean that the very composite saga, rather than the lay, has swerved from the original conception. It will also be observed that the poem is purely dialogic. Both action and motivation, and the description of the nightly scene of dread and gloom, are skillfully and completely achieved by this technique; so that, as in the best ballads, any prose introduction is supererogatory.

The lay has been justly admired.[1] There is power and subtlety in the portrayal of the amazon maiden. She is self-centered and undaunted, come what may, and ruthless in her fierce insistence ou fulfilling her destiny—"little reck I, ruler of men, whether my sons slay each other"—yet withal a strength girt round with weakness. Once she holds the coveted sword in her hand she flees to her ships, unnerved by the horrors of the night. Still the lay is decidedly in the later manner, in style and composition, and can hardly be older than, say, the twelfth century. The text, in regular *fornyrthislag,* is complete, though there seems to be some confusion in the order of the stanzas. It is found in the two main MSS of the *Hervarar saga*.

From the saga we learn that after the battle with Hiálmar and Orvar Odd on Sáms-isle, the latter interred Angantýr and his brothers in a barrow with all their weapons. Before his death Angantýr had begotten a daughter, Hervor. Like him, she was strong, fierce, and intractable. She wore armor like a man and joined a band of vikings whose chief she soon became. She lays her course to Sáms-isle to win Tyrfing, the wondrous sword. Alone she goes on land.

Old Norse Poems

1[2]   * * *

The SHEPHERD said:

"Who by himself hath come hither on isle?
Go thou straightway, get thee shelter!"

HERVOR said:

2 "I care not go and get me shelter:
not any one know I of the island's men.
Ere hence thou hiest, in haste tell me:
where are the howes for Hiorvarth[3] named?"

The SHEPHERD said:

3 "Ask not of such, if sage thou art,
friend-of-vikings:[4] thou 'rt on ferly ways;
let us fare hence so fast as feet will carry!
Without now is it awful for men."

HERVOR said:

4 "This trinket's thine if thou tell me this:
't were hard to hold back the heroes'-friend."[4]

The SHEPHERD said:

"Thou canst not give such golden trinkets,
such fair-shining rings, that I fare with thee.

5   "Tis folly, in faith, to fare thither
for a man alone in this murky dark:
is fire abroad, the barrows open,
burn field and fen: let us flee in haste."

HERVOR said:

6   "I scorn to dread a din like this,
though fires do burn all about the isle!
Let not men who are dead unman us, shepherd,
with fear so swiftly, but say thou on!"

The SHEPHERD said:

7   "Is Hel's gate lifted, the howes do ope,
the edge of the isle is all afire—
awful is it to be without:
to thy ships hie thee in haste, oh maiden!"

Old Norse Poems

HERVOR said:

8 "Such nightly blaze ye cannot build
   that of their fires afraid I grow:
   will Hervor's heart not be horror-struck,
   e'en though a ghost in grave-door stood.7

9 "Awake, Angantýr! Wakes thee Hervor,
   thy only bairn, born to Sváva;
   the bitter brand from thy belt gird thou,
   which swinking dwarfs for Svafrlami wrought.

10 "Hervarth, Hiorvarth, Hrani,8 Angantýr!
   I awake you all, ye wights neath mold
   with helmets and byrnies and bitter swords,
   with gory spears and all gear of war.

11 "Have Arngrím's sons, the evil men's,
   their corpses become to clay and mold,9
   seeing that none of the sons of Eyfura10
   with me will speak in Munar Bay.

12 "May all of you feel within your ribs
   as though in ant-hill your ill bones rotted,11
   but the sword ye fetch me forged by Dvalin:12
   it befits not ghosts to guard prized arms."

ANGANTÝR said:

13 "Hervor, daughter, why doest call me
with cold curses? They will cost thee dear!
Bereft of reason and raving art thou,
that with wildered thought thou wak'st the dead.

14 "Neither father me buried nor fellow kinsmen:
(thy brothers' banesmen this barrow raised.[13])
The twain who lived did Tyrfing win—
now one of the victors wields it at last."

HERVOR said:

15 "Thou say'st not sooth! May so the gods
leave thee whole in howe as thou hast not
Tyrfing with thee:[14] unwilling art
to give thy daughter her dearest wish."

ANGANTÝR said:

16[15] "Hardly human I hold thee, maiden,
about barrows who hoverest at night,
with graven spear[16] and Gothic iron,[17]
with helmet and byrnie, the hall's[18] gate before,

Old Norse Poems

HERVOR said:

17 "Howbeit, human was I held to be
ere hither I hied me, your hall to seek:
out of whose hand me the hater-of-byrnies,[19]
the dwarfs' handiwork: 't will not do to hide it!"

ANGANTÝR said:

18 "Under my shoulders hidden lies Hjálmar's bane,
about its blade blazes fire:
in this wide world know I no woman born
who would dare to wield the dreaded sword."

HERVOR said:

19 "Would I hold in hand— if have it I might—
the bitter brand, and in battle wield it,
Not a whit fear I the fire blazing:
it swiftly sinks as I seek it with eye."

ANGANTÝR said:

20 "I tell thee, Hervor— heed my warning!—
what will happen, thou heroes' daughter!
I say but sooth: will this sword become
the slayer of all thy sib and kin."

HERVOR said:

21 "Thus shall I deal with you dead men's bones
that in your graves ye get no rest:20
hand me, Angantýr, out of the howe
the sword wherewith thou slewest Hjálmar!"

ANGANTÝR said:

22 "Witless art thou, and of wanton mind,
like a fool to fling thee into fire blazing!
Out of howe, rather, shall I hand the sword,
hardy maiden, nor withhold it from thee."

HERVOR said:

23 "Well then doest thou, warriors'-offspring,
out of the howe to hand Tyrfing
which liefer to me, thou lord-of-battle,
than now to have all Norroway."

ANGANTÝR said:

24 "Thou little knowest, luckless woman,
what ill thou'st wrought with reckless speech:
I say but sooth: will this sword become
the slayer of all thy sib and kin."

HERVOR said:

25 "To my ships on shore now shall I hie me:
is the hero's daughter happy in mind.
Little reck I, ruler of men,
whether my sons will slay each other."

ANGANTÝR said:

26 "Thou 'lt have it through life and long joy in it;
but keep thou hidden Hjálmar's-slayer,
nor touch its edges: on the twain is poison.
Is that bitter brand baneful to all.

27 "Thou 'lt have a son who hereafter
will wield Tyrfing and trust his strength;
Heithrek[21] will he be hight of men,
and mightiest grow of men under heaven.

28 "Farewell, daughter! I would fain give thee
the thews of twelve men if thou 'ldst but heed me—
their lives and strength, the stored-up wealth
which Arngrím's sons left after them."

HERVOR said:

29 "Shall I hie me hence. Happily may ye—
I long to be gone— live in your howe.
But lately I lingered 'twixt life and death,[22]
when all about me blazed the fires."

Footnotes

[1] Though one will hardly agree with that otherwise so sane and sagacious observer, W. P. Ker, that "after *Voluspó* it is the most wonderful of Northern poems." *Epic and Romance,* p. 73.

[2] The *Hauksbók* MS has pieced out the missing lines with this introductory (narrative) half-stanza:

> Met the young maid in Munar Bay
> with setting of sun, a swain by his herd.

Munar Bay is a fictitious locality recalling the Una Bay in the *First Lay of Helgi,* 32.

[3] One of Angantýr's brothers, interred with him in the grave-mound (howe, barrow).

<u>4</u> Kenning for "warrior."

<u>5</u> A difficult stanza. I have followed the interpretation of the Prose in the distribution of the rôles; which, to be sure, involves the interpretation of *eigi* as the first person singular subjunctive of *eiga*.

<u>6</u> This and the following stanza-duplicating 5 and 6 — have been transposed here from their original position (in MSS after 13) notwithstanding the obvious difficulty of Hervor's true name and sex being mentioned: they grievously interpose there between Hervor's accusation and Angantýr's justification. Stanza 8 may be taken as spoken by Hervor to herself.

<u>7</u> In *Hauksbók*, the following weak stanza supplies the context:

> To the forest fast fled then the shepherd,
> nor more cared he to the maiden to speak;
> but hardier Hervor's her heart then swelled
> in derring-do, disdainfully—

"and went through the fires as though ther were but smoke, until she came to the barrow of the berserkers."

<u>8</u> Three of Angantýr's brothers.

<u>9</u> *I.e.*, have undergone the "second death," complete annihilation; until which time, popular belief held, the dead inhabited their graves in the form of spooks. This is to be remembered also against the stanzas following.

<u>10</u> Sváfrlami's daughter whom Arngrím had abducted by force.

11 Cf. the curses of Búsla.

12 One of the two dwarfs who forged Tyrfing for Sváfrlami.

13 The lacuna (not indicated in the MSS) is supplied here after the excellent suggestion of S. Bugge—Hiálmar and Orvar Odd (Sóti) or, rather, the latter alone.

14 Hervor wishes him everlasting life in his grave-mound if he had not the sword—as she is sure he has! In the original the stanza is not quite clear.

15 For the following stanzas, I adopt Genzmer-Heusler's arrangement.

16 *I.e.,* with a spear in whose iron figures, or characters, (of silver) were inlaid.

17 Indefinite kenning for "sword" or "armor."

18 Here for the burial chamber of the barrow.

19 Kenning for "sword,"

20 In the original, "that ye shall lie dead with spooks," which makes little sense. The stanza is imperfectly transmitted—with an excrescent long-line—and the translation therefore only an approximation.

21 Cf. The *Lay of Hloth* and *Angantýr,* Prose, and note.

22 *I.e.,* the realms of Life and Death.

Old Norse Poems

The Lay of Hloth and Angantýr

OR

The Battle of the Huns

This dialogic lay about the hostile half brothers may justly claim high rank among the small number of genuine "heroic" poems. In grandeur of theme, in extraordinary vigor and splendor of style, in heroic passion, it challenges comparison with such poems as *Atlakvitha* and *Hamthismól;* which it resembles also in its air of antiquity, in the epic-dramatic form, in the rugged mixture of *fornyrthtslag* and *málaháttr* and, alas! also in the sadly mutilated condition of the text. Fully one-third of the original poem seems lost, and a number of stanzas are no doubt corrupted. The total impression is much weakened by the connecting prose, which, in this case, to a large extent represents imperfectly remembered stanzas, with still an occasional rhythm, here and there an alliteration, or a striking phrase suggesting the noble original verse.

There are good reasons for thinking the lay a quasi-historical reminiscence from the time of Gothic greatness, transmitted possibly through some South Germanic song—partial reflection of the tremendous events of the migration period, perhaps the clash of Goth and Hun on the Catalaunian Fields (451), or some other vast battle of nations unrecorded in histories. The conflict is here located on the Dunheath, whether that locality be the plains of the Danube or those of the Lugii Duni about the upper Oder. In the latter case, it is interesting to note, the Jassar Fells (stanza 27) would correspond to the Jesenik (German, Gesenke), the stretch of hill country which forms the broad gate between the high and impassable Sudeti and the Carpathian ranges. This, again, would permit the inference that the Goths were at that time still in their North European homes by the Vistula[1] and the Baltic which, as we know from other sources, they right at the end of the second century A.D. Ultimate derivation from a Gothic lay of these remote times is no more impossible than in the case of *Hamthismól,* the great figures of Ermanaric and Theodoric, and their relations with Attila forming the very basic layer of Germanic folk hero lore. At any rate there are a number of clear indications that the lay has as its background the vast plains and broad rivers of the east central portions of Europe. Geographic exactness is not to be expected at that distance of time. A clear argument for the very early spread of the story may be seen in the fact that no less than five persons connected with it occur in lines 116-119 of the Anglo-Saxon catalogue poem of *Wīdsīth* from the seventh century—a poem which also otherwise betrays considerable knowledge of very early Continental conditions.

No doubt the episode here celebrated is the original kernel of the composite *Hervarar saga* in which it is preserved. For the lay after stanza 11 (of this translation) we are dependent on seventeenth-century MSS of the saga.

On one of his expeditions the evil but wise son of Hervor, King Heithrek, abducts the daughter of the powerful Humli,[2] King of the Huns. She gives birth to Hloth, who is brought up by his maternal grandfather, since Heithrek put his mother away in favor of another queen whose children by him are Angantýr and Hervor—a quasi reincarnation of her amazon grandmother. When Heithrek dies Angantýr succeeds him; but his half brother claims an equal share of the inheritance.

1 Of yore, say they, Humli[3] over Huns held sway;
Gizur[4] over Gauts;[5] over Goths, Angantýr;
Valdar over Danes, but over the Welsh,[6] Kíar;[7]
and Alrek[8] the Bold over English folk.

2 Was Hloth[9] born there in Hunnish folk-lands—
[10]with dagger and broadsword and byrnie long,
with ring-decked helmet[11] and sharp-hewing sword,
with horses well-broken, in the hallowed land.[12]

Now[13] Hloth learned about the death of his father, and that his brother, Angantýr, had himself made king over all those lands which Heithrek had owned. Then King Humli advised Hloth to claim from Angantýr his share of the inheritance with fair words; as is said here:

3 Rode Hloth from the East, King Heithrek's first-
born,
to the halls where dwell the dauntless Goths—
to Árheimar[14]— to claim his heir-lands.
There was Angantýr drinking arvel for Heithrek.

4   Before the high hall he found a hero standing,
    from far lands hailing, him he welcomed.15

    ## Hloth said:

    "Into high hall now go thou, hero,
    and bid Angantýr make answer to me."

The warrior went in before the table of King Angantýr, and said:

5   "Is Hloth come here, King Heithrek's heir,
    thy bastard brother, thy brother he;
    high the young hero his horse doth sit:
    would he now, thane, with thee have speech."

But when King Angantýr heard this, he threw down his trencher on the board and rose and clad himself in his byrnie. He took his white shield in hand, and grasped the sword Tyrfing with the other. Then there arose much din in the hall; as is here said:

6   Rose outcry in hall; with the atheling stood up,
(the Gothic king, his goodly warriors:[16])
they all fain would hear what Hloth did say,
and eke what answer Angantýr made.

ANGANTÝR said:

7   "Hail to thee, Hloth, King Heithrek's son
and my own brother! On bench sit thou!
In his hall let us drink Heithrek's arvel
[the father of us, the first of mankind]
in wine or in mead— whiche'er worthiest seemeth."[17]

HLOTH said:

8   "Not hither came we from Hunnish lands
to share with you your wine and mead—

* * *

9   "The half will I have of what Heithrek owned,
of awl[18] and of edge, of all the treasure,
of cow and of calf, of quern harsh-grinding,
of thrall and of bond-maid, and those born of them,

Old Norse Poems

10   the mighty forest which is Murkwood[19] hight,
the hallowed grave[20] which in Gothland stands,
the shining stone which in Danpstead[21] stands,
half of the war-weeds which Heithrek owned,
of lands and lieges and of lustrous arm-rings."

ANGANTÝR said:

11   "Your shining shield will be shattered, brother,
and by cold spears will be split many another,
[and many a man will meet his death]
before Tyrfing in two I sunder,
or to thee, son of Humli,[22] leave the half of it!

12   "Will I give thee, brother, gleaming arm-rings,
much wealth of gold, what most thou wishest—
twelve hundred thralls, twelve hundred steeds,
twelve hundred bond-men with bucklers weaponed.

13   "To every man of you much will I give—
other and better things than ere this he had:
to every man a maid will I give,
and give each maiden a golden necklace.

14   "About thee a-sitting shall I silver heap,
about thee a-going shall I gold-trinkets pour,[23]
so that the rings will roll about thee;
shalt govern a third[24] of Gothic lands."

Gizur, called the Follower[25] of the Grytings, King Heithrek's faster father, was then in Angantýr's company. He was exceeding old then. When he heard Angantýr's offer he thought that too much was offered, and said:

15   "Could no better be offered   to a bond-woman's son—
     to the son of a bond-woman,   though born to a king.
     The bastard son then   sate on a hill
     when the atheling   the heirlooms shifted."[26]

(Hloth is enraged and returns to Humli, who promises help for the summer after.)[27]

Humli said:

16   "Shall we feast at our ease   till over is winter,
     drink and hold converse,   quaffing the mead,
     and teach our warriors   weapons to fashion,
     which to battle bravely   we shall bear forward.

17 "Well shall we arm the warrior host,
and help thee, Hloth, with hardy deeds;28
with twelve-year old draughts, and two-year old foals,29
thus shall the host of the Huns be gathered."

That winter, King Humli and Hloth stayed at home; but when spring came they drew together so great a host that there was a dearth of fighting men in Hunland. . . . And when this mighty host was gathered they rode through Murkwood. . . . As they came out of the forest they found many farms and level fields. In the fields there stood a fair castle. There ruled Hervor, Angantýr's and Hloth's sister, and with her, Ormar, her foster father. They warded the land against the Huns and had a great host. . . . One morning, about sunrise, Hervor stood on a tower above the castle gate. She saw so much dust southward toward the forest that it hid the sun for a long time. Then saw she a glow under the dust, as though from gold, of fair shields inlaid with gold, of gilded helmets and bright byrnies. Then understood she that this was the Hunnish host, and most numerous. She hurried down and called her trumpeter and bade him summon the host. Then said Hervor to them: "Take your weapons and make ready for battle; but thou, Ormar, ride out toward the

Huns and affer them battle before the southern gate."[30]

ORMAR[31] said:

18   "Assuredly shall I, with shield aloft,
     (to the Hunnish host hurriedly ride,
     to summon them to the southern gate)[32]
     there 'gainst the Goths to try the game of war."

(And so he did and) then returned to the castle. Then was Hervor armed and all her host. . . . There was a great battle; but because the Huns had a much greater host, the battle turned against Hervor, and at length she fell, and round about her, many men. But when Ormar saw her fall he fled, and with him all they who still lived. He rode day and night as fast as he could, to King Angantýr in Árheimar, while the Huns took to harrying and burning the countryside. When he arrived he said:

19   From the south am I come, to say these tidings:
     burned is the far-famed forest Murkwood,
     all Goth-land drenched with the gore of the fallen.

20   "I know that Hervor, Heithrek's daughter,
and thy sister, by the sword has fallen.
Have Hunnish hosts hewed down the maiden
with many an other of your warriors.

21   * * *
Was she readier for war than with wooer to dally,
or on bench to sit as wedded bride."

When Angantýr heard this he stroked his beard and was silent for a long time. At last he said:

22   "Wast unbrotherly dealt with, my brave sister!
(Now have fallen the fighters who fared with you.)[33]
Full many the men when mead we drank,—
have I fewer followers when I fain would have more.

23   "In all my host no hero see I,
though I should beg him and buy him with rings,
who would raise the war-shield and ride for me
to the Hunnish host to harbinger war.

Lee M. Hollander

GIZUR THE OLD said:

24 "Not a single silverling seek I of thee,
nor of glistening gold guerdon crave I;
yet shall I ride and raise the war-shield,
and to Hunnish hosts herald battle."

It was King Heithrek's law, that if a hostile army was in the land and the king of the land challenged them to a pitched battle and appointed the battle field, then those vikings durst not harry before battle was tried between them. Gizur then armed himself with good weapons and leaped on his horse as though he were a young man, and said to the king:[34]

"To the Huns where shall I herald battle?"

ANGANTÝR said:

25 "On the down of Dun-heath and in Dylgia[35]-vales
(shall the battle be)[36] 'neath the Iassar-fells' brow,
where often Goths their glaives reddened,
and victory won warriors in sword-play."

Then Gizur rode till he came upon the Hunnish army. When he was within earshot he called out with a loud voice and said:

* * *
* * *

26 "Afraid are your hosts, fey is your leader—
You have angered Othin: we offer you battle.

27 "On the downs of Dun-heath and in Dylgia-vales
I bid you battle, 'neath the Iassar-fells' brow.
(May Othin o'erawe Angantýr's foes)[37]
and may this spear fly o'er you as I do bid it."[38]

When Hloth had heard Gizur's words he said:

28 "Seize ye Gizur (the Grýtings' follower),[39]
Angantýr's man, from Árheimar come!"

Humli said:

29 ("No hurt nor harm to him shall be done,
to hero who fares to herald us war."

GIZUR said:

"Will not Hunnish hornbows do harm to us ever,
nor Hunnish wiles hinder our warriors."[40]

Gizur then gave the spurs to his horse and rode back to King Angantýr. . . . The king asked him whether he had encountered the Huns. Gizur said: I spoke with them and summoned them to combat

"on the downs of Dun-heath and in Dylgia-vales."

Angantýr asked him how great an army the Huns had. Gizur said:

"Huge was that host (of Hunnish warriors)

30 "Sixteen squadrons[41] saw I foregathered;
had each squadron fully five thousand men,
and each 'thousand,'[42] thirteen hundred,
and each 'hundred,' horse-men eight-score."

Angantýr then got together an army to meet the Huns, who were twice his strength. The battle lasted eight days, with great slaughter which was made good, in the case of the Goths, by continual reinforcements; so that at last the Huns were forced to give ground. Angantýr stepped into the front ranks with the sword Tyrfing in hand, and slew both Hloth and Humli. Then the Huns took to flight, and the Goths slew so many that the rivers were dammed up and overflowed their banks and the valleys were filled with dead men and horses. Angantýr went about on the battlefield to search among the fallen. He found his brother Hloth. Then he said:

31 "Untold arm-rings I offered thee, brother,
    a wealth of gold and what most thou didst wish.
    As guerdon for strife now hast gotten neither,
    nor lands nor lieges nor lustrous rings.

32 "A baleful fate wrought it that, brother, I slew thee!
    Will that aye be told. Ill's the norns' doom."

Footnotes

<u>1</u> In *Wīdsīth* (ll. 119 f) we are told that the Goths defended their ancient home against the Huns "about the forest of the Vistula."

<u>2</u> In whom we may see the representative of the royal race of the Ostrogoths, the Amalunga, who for a time were subjects, or allies, of the Huns; and in Heithrek, *Hardurík* (*Ardaricus*), king of the Gepidæ, a tribe related to the Goths, who fought heroically against the Huns.

<u>3</u> This stanza is held by some not to belong to the lay.

<u>4</u> Pronounce Gitsur. Cf. the Prose after 14.

<u>5</u> Old Norse *Gautar*, the inhabitants of the present Swedish provinces of East and West Gotland. Not to be confused with the Goths (Old Norse *Gotar*)—a name frequently used in a general and honorific, but here in a special, sense. The seats, at different times, of that noble and gifted race ranged from the Baltic to the Black Sea and thence to Spain.

<u>6</u> Used, vaguely, of various west and south European nations.

<u>7</u> This name is by some scholars held to be derived from Cæsar, in view especially of *Wīdsīth,* lines 76-78—*mid Cāsere, sē the wimburga geweald āhte, Wiolena and Wilna and Wala rīces.*

<u>8</u> No such English king is known in legend or history. The name seems identical with that of Abbot Ælfric, the famous writer of the latter part of the tenth century; but unconsciously one thinks of Alfred the Great (849-901).

9 The hostile brothers no doubt correspond to the *Hlithe* and *Incgentheōw* of *Wīdsīth*. *Leth* was the third king of the Langobardians.

10 Thus Helgi "stands in arms" in earliest infancy; cf. the *First Lay of Helgi*. The prose preceding rationalizes this heroic trait as follows: "It was said, in former times, that a man was born 'with weapons and horses,' for the reason that the weapons lay ready when he was born—also livestock, such as oxen and horses, if they happened to be born then. All these were given at birth to men of rank, to honor them."

11 I.e., helmets adorned with strips of plaited rings, as were used in the Viking period.

12 I.e., within the confines of royal residence and temple.

13 This prose link may possibly paraphrase the contents of a lost stanza or stanzas. Still, bearing in mind the abrupt transitions in ballad technique, we need not conclude this.

14 I.e., "River-Dwelling"; by some supposed to be by the Dniepr River, about which lay the lands of the Goths in the fourth century.

15 Very evidently, it is Hloth who comes from afar; but the text is ambiguous. To judge from similar passages in other poems, a half-stanza containing a question of the warrior on guard, and one containing the beginning of Hloth's speech, are missing.

16 The gap supplied after the suggestion of Heusler-Ranisch.

17 This stanza and the following half-stanza are found only in one seventeenth century MS. However, it expresses the substance rather better than the Prose.

18 Thus the text. Possibly, the awl is taken as representative of peaceful pursuits. "Edge," *pars pro toto* for "sword."

19 This great forest is mentioned also in the *Lay of Atli*, 8, and in the *Plaint of Oddrún*, 23, as separating the land of the Niflungs from that of the Huns.

20 Bugge (*Norrœne Skrifter*, etc.) suggests that the "hallowed grave" refers to a burial place where the departed Gothic kings were interred; and the "shining stone," to a boulder in the high place of assembly of the Goths on which the newly chosen kings were acclaimed by the people.

21 I.e., "Stead by the Dniepr" (Latin Danaper), probably. It is mentioned also in *Rígsthula*.

22 I.e., his daughter's son.

23 Cf. the penalty paid by the gods for killing Otter, *Reginsmól*.

24 Which is the usual share, according to Old Germanic law, of the son born out of wedlock.

25 Here equivalent to "armor-bearer" — as is, e.g., Hildebrand to Dietrich. The Grytings are probably identical with the Ostrogoths, by the Latin and Greek authors called *Greothingi, Grouthingoi* (Bugge, *op. cit.*). As the wicked adviser and instigator of strife, he may represent Óthin. His name may be a reminiscence of the East Germanic name Geiseric (Gizericus).

26 He sarcastically implies that Hloth would acknowledge himself to be a bastard, entitled to compensation — and no more — if he accepted anything but half of his inheritance. Hloth is likened to a shepherd on a hill, tending his flocks, when the kingdom was divided.

Old Norse Poems

27 The wordy prose link of the original no doubt represents one or more stanzas now lost.

28 The half-line is uncertain.

29 *I.e.,* down to the last available resources in men and supplies.

30 This passage must represent a series of stanzas; the last one evidently in direct speech, to which the following stanza is the answer.

31 The *Wyrmhere* of *Wīdsīth*.

32 The missing half-stanza is supplied following the suggestions of Bugge and Heusler-Ranisch.

33 Freely supplied by the translator after the suggestion of the prose.

34 The last sentence of the prose no doubt paraphrases the lost portion of this stanza.

35 "Battle." Name of a traditional field of battle?

36 Supplied for this corrupt half line.

37 Supplied freely by the translator for a hopelessly corrupt line.

38 Thus dedicating them to Óthin; cf. *Voluspó*.

39 Supplied by all editors.

40 Both half-stanzas tentatively restored by the translator from the prose.

41 Conjectural.

42 "Hundreds" and "thousands" are here used as designations for smaller tactical units.

Old Norse Poems

The Lay of Innstein

This Lay is found in the mythic-heroic *Hálfs saga*, a typical *fornaldarsaga*, or "tale of the olden times," consisting of narrative with interspersed poems, which in this instance preponderate. The prose is largely commentary, or furnishes connecting links, for the many *lausavísur* ("single stanzas") and other poems that make up the bulk of the saga.[1] Indeed, in our lay it might be dispensed with altogether, for the action is admirably brought out in the dialogue and ensuing monologue. Though pleasing in invention and smooth in diction and versification (*fornyrthislag*), the stereotyped phrasing and evident borrowings from such older poems as *Biarkamól*, Vikarsbálk, and perhaps, *Atlamól*, betray its late origin (thirteenth century). Only one stanza, the sixteenth, stands out in peculiar vigor as though a remnant of some nobler edifice.

The saga deals chiefly with the life of the famous sea-king Hálf and his chosen band, the *Hálfsrekkiar*. When after eighteen years of Viking life, he returns with his fleet to his native kingdom of Horthaland, his stepfather, Ásmund, who had ruled it in his stead, feigns submission and invites Hálf to his hall with half his company; and he accepts, against the earnest warnings of Innstein, his old companion at arms. They are made drunk, the hall is fired over their heads; but the heroes rouse themselves and break out of the hall. In the struggle outside they fall to a man, not wishing to survive their beloved leader; at least, this is clearly the intention of the lay. A later poet, to be sure, allowed several of Hálf's men to escape and avenge him in time. About them, we have in the saga the lays of Útstein[2] and of Hrók, in a somewhat similar vein.

Old Norse Poems

INNSTEIN said:

1 "Up to Ásmund would all of us
from our dragons hie them,— most doughty men:
In their hall let us burn the host of warriors,
and send to Hel Ásmund's heroes!"

HÁLF said:

2 "Let half, only, of our host
on our errand to Ásmund fare:
hath he offered us, most open-handed,
many wroughten rings of reddish gold."

INNSTEIN said:

3 "You guess not, ring-giver, the guile of Ásmund:
is that crafty king cunning in mind.
If, war-lord, thou our warning heedest,
put little faith in thy stepfather!"

HÁLF said:

4 "Hath Ásmund sworn oaths full many,
and made pledges, as men do know:
will a good liege not give the lie to his oaths,
nor one atheling the other bewray."

INNSTEIN said:

5 "Hath Óthin grown angry with thee,
   since all too well thou Ásmund trustest:
   by wicked wiles he will undo us,
   unless on guard against him art!"

HÁLF said:

6 "Aye words of fear art fain to utter:
   that prince will not thus break his pledge.
   Gold we'll get there, and goodly things
   to have and to hold, from his hoard of rings."

INNSTEIN said:

7 "This dream had I— to heed it were wise!—
   that flames flickered fiercely about us,
   whence hard was it to hack our way.
   What deem'st thou, king, this dream betokens?"[3]

HÁLF said:

8 "A guilded helmet shall I give to each
   of the fearless heroes that follow me:
   would they seem to flash as though fire did blaze
   on the hair-hillocks[4] of the hardy men."

Old Norse Poems

INNSTEIN said:

9 "Still another dream I after had:
that fire methought to flame on my shoulders;
I guess that little good it bodeth.
What deem'st thou, king, this dream betokens?"

HÁLF said:

10 "Golden byrnies on the backs rattle
of war-workers who in wedges array them:5
the shield-bearers' shoulders they will shine upon,
bright to behold like blazing fire."

INNSTEIN said:

11 "A third time still I this did dream:
that in deepest sea we had sunk together;
great tidings this must betoken.
What deem'st thou, king, this dream bodeth?"

HÁLF said:

12 "Be done with dreams and doting talk:
I deem that naught thy dreams betoken.
Say thou no more in my hearing
of these thy dreams from this day onward."

INNSTEIN said:

13 "Ye Hrók brothers, in the host of the king,
    and Útstein eke: I utter warning!
    Let all of us go up to the hall,
    and listen not to the liege's words!"

ÚTSTEIN said:

14 "Our brave chieftain shall choose for us,
    the foremost in war, how fare we shall:
    as the liege liketh so let us, brother,
    risk our lives now and the leader follow!"

INNSTEIN said:

15 "Did our lord listen, in the wars as we lay,
    many a time to my counsel;
    but now, ween I, he will in naught
    give heed to me, since hither we came."

Then went King Hálf with the half of his ship company to the hall of King Ásmund. There they found a great host. Great plenty reigned at the feast, and the drink was so strong that Hálf's men fell fast asleep. King Ásmund and his men set fire to the hall. Then said Innstein:

Old Norse Poems

16 "There's smoke o'er hawks[6] in the hall of the king:
I wait me the drip of wax from swords.[7]
'Tis time to deal out treasure and gold
among Hálf's heroes, and helmets eke.

17 "That would I now that Hálf awake:
are fires kindled unquenchable.
To Ásmund oughtest, wise atheling,
to the grim-minded, his gifts requite.[8]

18 "Let us bravely batter the beer-hall's walls!
Gape even now the gable walls;
will ever be sung, while earth lasteth,
how Hálf's heroes hardily fared.

19 "Briskly forward, nor back a foot!
Will the war-workers[9] have to wield their swords:
will themselves be seared with sore gashes
and sore wounds, ere the battle is stilled.

20 "Let the warriors wend their way quickly
out of the fire with the atheling!
Forever liveth not any man:
will the folk-warder not fear to die."

It is told that King Hálf and his men made their way out of the blazing hall and that he was overwhelmed by the greater host outside—he and his men. When the king was fallen, Innstein said:

21. "Here saw I all, equally bold,
    fearlessly follow the folk-warder:
    well met, again, when after we meet[10]
    Than death, life is not lighter to bear!"

Then those men joined the fray who had stayed by the ships. There fell many of Hálf's warriors. The battle lasted till night, ere Innstein fell. He said:

22. "Is Hrok fallen with Hálf the king—
    the fearless one at the feet of his lord;
    but ill owe we to Óthin now
    who overthrew a thane so brave.

23. "Eighteen summers[11] I did follow
    the ruler, roving, to redden spears;
    no other king eager for war
    shall I ever have, to grow old with him.

24. "Will Innstein here to the earth sink dead,
    whole-hearted henchman, by the head of his king.
    will men e'er after to mind call it
    that laughing died this lord of men."

Old Norse Poems

Footnotes

1 As, e.g., in the *Reginsmól-Fáfnismól* of the Edda.

2 As to the names of Innstein and his brother, Útstein, they seem to be connected with the royal estate of Útstein in Horthaland; cf. *Haraldskvæthi* 9 and note.

3 Cf. the dreams of Kostbera, *Atlamól*, 4 ff.

4 Kenning for "head."

5 Reference is here made to the wedge formation favored by many Germanic tribes in battle.

6 *I.e.*, "warriors."

7 Swords were dipped in wax to protect them against rust (and witchcraft).

8 Ironic allusion to fires kindled for the welcome, and presents given at the departure, of guests.

9 Ásmund's men.

10 *I.e.*, after death, in Valholl.

11 The Viking expeditions took place only in summer.

Lee M. Hollander

Old Norse Poems

HILDIBRAND'S DEATH SONG

THIS FINE fragment is an offshoot of the South Germanic, and ultimately Gothic, heroic motif best known to us from the famous old German lay in which the greatest tragedy conceivable to the Germanic mind, kinsman slain by kinsman—son by father—has found classic expression. There, Hiltibrant, the grey-haired warrior, returning from long exile, meets his fiery young son Hadubrant, recognizes, and makes advances to him but is rebuffed and, to save his honor, is compelled to fight and slay him. In the Old Norse poem it is Hildibrand who is slain, by his half brother, Ásmund; and the previous death of Hildibrand's son at his own hands (stanza 6) is right only as a kind of rudiment. The lay is found, in a much mutilated condition, in the *Asmunda saga kappabana* ("the Saga of Ásmund, Slayer of Champions"), a *fornaldarsaga* which must have existed in the twelfth century about as it has come down to us, since it is found in a very similar form in Saxo's *Danish History*[1] which was composed toward the end of that century. This version also contains a Latin paraphrase of the lay, in hexameters, agreeing with our fragment down to verbal details; so that a tentative reconstruction of certain lines and stanzas is justifiable.

101

The saga tells how King Buthli's daughter, Hild—in the lay and in Saxo she is called Drótt—by the fortunes of war is married successively to two kings. Her sons by these, Hildibrand and Ásmund,[2] grow up in ignorance of one another. Both become great warriors. Hildibrand is attached to the Hunnish court, Ásmund becomes the champion of two Saxon lords whose realm has been reduced by Hildibrand. He takes up Hildibrand's standing challenge to single combat; but as Hildibrand through a description has recognized Ásmund he avoids him and sends his berserkers instead. Only when these have all succumbed does he issue forth himself to the struggle which he knows will be fatal to one or both of them. Wounded unto death, Hildibrand addresses the victor:

Old Norse Poems

1   ("'Tis time to tell, on turf as I lie,
    felled by the sword, what fate was ours:
    unlike our lot in life hath been,
    to Hel fare I while whole thou livest.)[3]

2   "Not easy is it ever to know
    who will be born his brother's slayer.[4]
    Old Grótt bear thee in Danish lands;
    myself she bore in Sweden's realm.

3   ("By the same mother suckled we were;
    yet neither the other knew as brother
    until the twain, trusting their weapon,
    for the fray eager, fought the other:)[5]

4   "Trusty broad-swords twain were forged—
    heirlooms from Buthli; now one is broken.
    So deftly had the dwarfs forged them
    as none e'er did or will do, hereafter.[6]

5 "By my head, broken, my buckler stands,
 (round-shaped, shining, but shattered now;)[7]
 on it are scored eighty notches
 for doughty men given to death by me.

6 "My liefest son lies by my head,[8]
 the after-heir whom I did have—
    * * *
 unwittingly in war I slew him.

7 "One boon, brother, I beg of thee—
 one boon only albeit one
 which slayer not often to slain man grants:[10]
 in thy weeds of war wind my body!

8 "Have hateful norns knit our fate-thread:
 to fight against fate the fey one avails not;[11]
 lifeless shall I now lie on the ground,
 slain by the sword, sorely wounded."

According to the saga, Ásmund—ill-pleased with his deed—fulfills his brother's dying wish. But when he returns from the combat he scornfully remarks about the "odd custom" of sending two men against one.[12] Of the four stanzas put into his mouth, the fourth stands out with peculiar vigor.

Old Norse Poems

ASMUND said:

1   "I little bethought me of laws like these—[13]
    that me, single-handed, many would challenge
    when as their champion the Huns chose me,[14]
    eight times over, for the atheling's realm.

2   "I grappled with one, and again with two—
    with four and five of their followers;
    with six and seven at the same time, then,
    and one against eight: a wonder I live!

3   "But then wavered, wincing, my courage
    when eleven warriors me alone bestead,
    ere that in my sleep said to me wraiths[15]
    that I should dare to do battle.

4   "Then came the hoary[16] Hildibrand,
    the Hunnish warrior; nor he my match:[17]
    I marked on him, his helmet beneath,
    a deadly wound, dealt with the sword."[18]

Footnotes

1 Book VII.

2 In Saxo, Hildigerus and Halfdanus.

3 Supplied by the translator after Saxo, lines 1-7.

4 I accept E. A. Kock's emendation.

5 Do., after lines 10-16.

6 Two wondrous swords to which, however, a curse had been attached, had been forged for Buthli by two dwarfs. They came into the possession of the half brothers. In the duel, Hildibrand's is shattered.

7 Supplied after lines 18-19 of Saxo's paraphrase.

8 The recurrence of "by my head" renders the line suspicious. In Saxo's verses the dying Hildeglr's shield is adorned with the figures of the warriors he had slain—among them his own son: "in the middle (panel) stands the picture of my son, drawn with great art, whom this hand of mine snatched out of life." In the saga, Hildibrand is represented as slaying his son in the berserker rage which overcomes him before going to meet Ásmund.

8 There is nothing in Saxo's version to suggest a lacuna here.

10 It being customary, rather, that the victor despoils the vanquished of his armor.

11 Freely supplied by the translator after Saxo's lines 31-34.

12 Which is dishonorable, according to the code of the single combat.

13 Adopting Detter's and Heinzel's emendation of the passage.

14 The strange contradiction in this line might, possibly, be interpreted ironically as meaning that they picked him as their opponent.

15 In the original *dísir,* tutelary spirits in the shape of women, guiding and warning one.

16 This epithet shows the same, older, conception as the *Lay of Hiltibrant* where Hiltibrant is called "*alter Hun*"; whereas in the saga he is represented as youthful, notwithstanding his having a grown son.

17 Or "hard to overcome." The line seems corrupt.

18 F. Jónsson's emendation.

Lee M. Hollander

Old Norse Poems

The Lay of Harold

[HARALDSKVÆTHI OR HRAFNSMÓL] BY THÓRBIORN HORNKLOFI

NORWAY enters into the full daylight of recorded history with King Harold, surnamed Fairhair[1] (ca. 860-933), the son of Halvdan the Black, a petty king of Southeastern Norway. While still a youth, Harold after a bitter struggle with the independence-loving nobles brought the whole realm under his sway. The final victorious battle, against a coalition of chieftains of the West reinforced by auxiliaries from the British Isles, was a naval action fought in the Hafrs-firth (873), an inlet of southwest Norway. It is celebrated in this lay. After this battle, rather than submit and pay tribute to Harold, many nobles left the land with all their kin and possessions, settling in the Western Isles and, chiefly, in Iceland.

Among the engaging qualities of this masterful ruler must be reckoned his fondness for poetry. We are told in the reliable *Egils saga* that "of all his followers, he valued most his skalds,"[2] thus probably initiating the tradition of court poets that lasted for centuries. In fact, he is said to have been a poet in his own right, like many of his successors. Several of his court poets are named in the sagas and represented by poems. Of Thórbiorn hornklofi's[3] personality we know little, except that he was of high birth and "an old friend of kings, who had always been attached to their courts." Two longer poems are attributed to him, the Glymdrápa,[4] a lay apparently descriptive of Harold's many battles before accomplishing the unification of Norway, thoroughly Skaldic in manner, which exists only in inconsiderable fragments; and the present poem, much simpler in style, which is given no name in the sources. This, the Haraldskvæthi or Hrafnsmól, as it has been called by some editors, is in a most deplorable condition.

As here given[5] it is pieced together from fragments found mainly in the large historical work called Fagrskinna,[6] which contains a history of the Norwegian kings. There is considerable difficulty about the authorship of these portions, some editors considering stanzas 7 to 11, in particular, as a separate poem dealing with the battle in the Hafrsfirth. The remainder, with descriptions of the life at Harold's court, is probably incomplete.

The structure of the poem is simple. After the usual admonition to the assembled court to lend their ears, the poet tells us what he heard a raven—scavenger of the battle-field—say to a valkyrie who questions him about Harold's deeds—naturally all warlike ones. For once, the scenes of carnage here described are individualized. There is grim Viking humor, a dramatic tension, a zest in these descriptions which one inevitably associates with a contemporary and participant.7 Upon her further questioning we are given realistic, even coarse-grained, glimpses of Harold's youth, his many marriages, and his life at court with berserkers, skalds, and jugglers. In all this, the poem is likely to have set the fashion; possibly also in the alternation of meters. The greater part is in sonorous *málaháttr*, smaller portions also in *lióthaháttr* and *fornyrthislag*.

1 Hearken, ye ring-bearers,8 while of Harold I tell you,
the mightily wealthy, and his manful war-deeds;
words I o'erheard a maiden high-minded speaking,
golden-haired, white-armed, with a glossy-beaked
raven.

2 Wise thought her the valkyrie; were welcome never
men9 to the bright-eyed one, her who birds' speech
knew well.
Greeted the light-lashed maiden, the lily-throated
woman,
the Hymir's-skull-cleaver10 as on cliff he was
perching.

3 "How is it, ye ravens— whence are ye come now
with beaks all gory, at break of morning?
Carrion-reek ye carry, and your claws are bloody.
Were ye near, at night-time, where ye knew of
corpses?"

4 Shook himself the dun-hued one, and dried his beak,
the eagle's oath-brother, and of answer bethought
him:
"Harold we follow, Halfdan's first-born,
I the young Yngling, since out of egg we crept.

Old Norse Poems

5   That king thou knowest, him who at Kvinnar[11] dwelleth,
    the hoard-warder of North men, who has hollow war-ships
    with reddish ribs[12] and with reddened war-shields,
    with tarred oar-blades and with tents[13] foam-besprinkled.

6   Fain outside[14] would he drink the ale at Yule-tide,[15]
    the fight-loving folk-warder, and Frey's[16]-game play there.
    Even half-grown, he hated the hearthfire cozy,
    the warm women's room, and the wadded down-mittens.[17]

7   Hearken how the high-born one in the Hafrs-firth[18] fought there,
    the keen-eyed king's son, against Kiotvi[19] the wealthy:
    came the fleet from the eastward,[20] eager for fighting,
    with gaping figureheads and graven ship-prows.[21]

8   "They were laden with franklins and lindenshields gleaming,
    with Westland spearshafts and with Welsh broadswords.
    The berserkers[22] bellowed as the battle opened,
    the wolf-coats[22] shrieked loud and shook their weapons.

9   "Their strength would they try, but he taught them to flee,
    the lord of the Eastmen[23] who at Útstein[24] dwelleth.
    The steeds-of-Nokkvi[25] he steered out when started the battle.
    Then boomed the bucklers ere a blow felled Haklang.[26]

10 "The thick-necked atheling behind the isle took shelter:
    he grew loath, against Lúfa[27] to hold the land of his fathers.
    Then hid under benches, and let their buttocks stick up,
    they who were wounded, but thrust their heads keelward.

Old Norse Poems

11 "Their shoulders shielded   the shifty heroes[28]—
were they showered with slung-shot— with the shingles-of-Gladhome.[29]
Home from Hafrs-firth hastened they eastward,
fled by way of Iathar,[30] of ale-cups thinking.[31]

12 "On the gravel lay the fallen, given to the one-eyed
husband of Fulla;[32] were we[33] fain of such doings.

13 "Of more and other things shall the maids of Ragnhild,[34]
the haughty women-folk, now have to gabble
than of the heath-dwellers[35] which Harold not ever
feasted on the fallen, as their friends had done oft.[36]

14 "The high-born liege-lord took the lady from Denmark—
broke with his Rogaland sweethearts and their sisters from Northaland,
with those from Heithmork and Hálogaland eke."[37]

THE VALKYRIE

15 "Whether is open-handed he-who-hastens-the-battle,[38]
to those who fend faithfully foemen from his homeland?"

THE RAVEN

16 "With much goods are gladdened the gallant warriors,
who in the hall of Harold while the time with chess-play:[39]
with much wealth he rewards them, and with well-forged broadswords,
with gold from Hunland[40] and with girls from the Eastfolks.[40]

17 "Most happy are they when there is hope for battle,
all ready to rouse them and to row strongly,[41]
so as to snap the thongs and to sunder the thole-pins,
to churn the brine briskly at the beck of their liege-lord."

THE VALKYRIE

18   "Of the skalds' lot would I ask thee, since thou skill
of that boastest:
how the bards fare there thou full well knowest—
      they who are in Harold's hall."

THE RAVEN

19   "Is seen from their raiment and their red-gold
finger-rings
      that a kind king they have.
Red fur-cloaks own they, most fairly bordered,
swords wound with silver,[42] and sarks ring-woven,[43]
gilded baldricks and graven helmets,
heavy gold bracelets which Harold bestowed on
them."

THE VALKYRIE

20   "Of the berserkers' lot would I ask thee, thou who
batten'st on corpses:
how fare the fighters who rush forth to battle,
      and stout-hearted stand 'gainst the foe?"

THE RAVEN

21   "Wolf-coats are they called, the warriors unfleeing,
        who bear bloody shields in battle;
  the darts redden where they dash into battle
        and shoulder to shoulder stand.
  'T is men tried and true only, who can targes shatter,
  whom the wise war-lord wants in battle."

THE VALKYRIE

22   "Of Andath and all his ilk, too, have I asked thee but little:
  how fare the fiddlers, how fare the jugglers
        in the halls of Harold?"

THE RAVEN

23   "His earless dog does your Andath fondle;
  the churl with his fool-tricks makes the folk-warder chuckle.
  Yet be there others who about the fire
        bowls of hot wine bear;
  their flapping fools'-caps they tuck fast in their belts—
        fellows you're free to kick."[44]

Footnotes

1 Concerning his name, cf. the note on stanza 10.

2 Their gratitude finds typical expression in stanza 19.

3 This surname probably means "raven" — given him with reference, it may be, to his most famous poem.

4 "War-alarum drápa (song of praise)."

5 I follow Finnur Jónsson's arrangement.

6 "Beautiful skin (Parchment)."

7 To be sure, it has been observed that the king could not be said to reside on the estates of Útstein and Kvinnar until some time after the conquest of the districts in which they are located.

8 Kenning for "warriors."

9 As lovers or husbands. The line is difficult.

10 According to *Grimnismól,* st. 40, the sky was made of the giant Hymir's skull. The raven cleaves the sky in his flight.

11 No such estate is known. Very likely, the famous royal farm on Ogvaldsnes, on the island of Karm (Rogaland), near the present town of Haugesund, is meant.

12 Adopting Finnur Jónsson's emendation.

13 The awnings under which the crew slept at night.

14 *I.e.,* at sea.

15 The great banquet and reunion, called the "Yule-ale," was held at the winter solstice.

16 Frey is the god of fertility and not associated with warfare. One should expect a valkyrie's name; but as it happens the text is clear, and no valkyrie's name begins with the alliterating F.

17 Or "pillows."

18 "Goat-firth," on the coast of the old district of Rogaland in southwestern Norway.

19 "The Fat"; which is supposed to be the nickname for King Guthrœth of Agthir.

20 That of the allies: owing to the lay of the land in Western Norway, "east" came frequently to be used for "south."

21 The warships of the Viking Age frequently had their stems and sterns carved in the likeness of a dragon's head and tail. Hence the term "dragon-ship."

22 Both designations for fierce warriors; cf. *Hárbarthslióth,* 37, note.

23 Harold, whose home dominions were in southeastern Norway.

24 This estate, like those mentioned above, is situated in southwestern Norway.

25 Nokkvi is the name of a mythical sea-king; his steed, therefore, is the "ship."

26 "Long-chin" (or "Long One with the Harelip"); which is thought to be the nickname for Ólaf the White, famous Viking chief of Dublin.

27 "Untidy shock of hair," Harold's nickname. The legend tells that, when rejected by the fair Gytha, as not being the lord of all Norway, he made the vow neither to cut nor comb his hair till he had brought the whole land under his sway, or else died. But after he had fulfilled his vow, and had it cut and cleansed, he was called "Hairfair," from his long silky hair.

28 *I.e.*, in fleeing.

29 *Glathsheimr* "the shining abode," the dwelling of Óthin in Valholl (see *Grimnismól,* stanza 8), is here substituted by the translator for *Sváfnis salnæfrar* "the-shingles-of-Óthin's-hall," *i.e.*, the shields with which (*ibid.*, stanza 9) the roof of Óthin's hall is covered.

30 The present Jæ(de)ren, the southwesternmost district of Norway.

31 *I.e.*, to be home again at their ease; but the interpretation is doubtful.

32 Óthin. Fulla, a hypostasis of Frigg, his wife, is substituted here by the translator.

33 *I.e.*, the ravens. There is the suspicion that something is lacking after this line.

34 The Danish princess who superseded Harold's many other wives.

35 *I.e.*, the wolves.

36 The meaning of this difficult stanza is, that the Danish women can now no longer taunt Harold for not having fed the wolves on the carcasses of the slain, *i.e.,* for not being warlike. It has been supposed that stanzas 13 and 14 may be fragments of another poem.

37 In order, these districts lie in the southeast, the west, the east center, and the north, of Norway. The order has been changed here.

38 The king.

39 Or, perhaps, the game referred to in *Heithrek's Riddles,* 26.

40 Here, probably generalized names.

41 It was by no means below the dignity of warriors to ply the oars in warships; cf. the situation in *Atlamól hin grœnlænzku,* stanza 34. The oar moved against a tholepin and was secured by thongs.

42 *I.e.,* the hilts, which were wound with silver wire.

43 *I.e.,* the shirts of mail.

44 The valkyrie rather falls out of her rôle in asking about Harold's jesters and jugglers. The raven voices the scorn generally felt, and expressed by the skalds, of the low buffoonery of these foreigners—for such they were generally— who competed with the skalds for the favors of their prince. The meaning of lines 3-5 is much debated. I follow S. Blöndal's recent suggestions.

Old Norse Poems

The Lay of Eric
[Eiríksmól]

THE MANUSCRIPT *Fagrskinna* is our sole source for this magnificent lay also. We are told that it was composed at the behest of Gunnhild, wife of Eric Bloody-axe, oldest of the many sons of Harold Hairfair, and his heir constituted. Driven by his half brother, Hákon the Good, from Norway where he was hated on account of his bloody deeds, Eric fled to England and carved himself a kingdom in Northumbria. From this, he was driven, too, and killed in a skirmish, it seems, in the year 950 according to the English Annals. A fierce and rough warrior, he had few redeeming features besides his bravery. He was baptized when acknowledging King Eadred of England as his overlord; but in this encomium of an unknown (Norwegian?) poet the heathen ethos prevails altogether: warfare as the great content of life.

The lay is generally regarded as a fragment; but that may be doubted, for the action seems clear and self-sufficient in its bold simplicity:

Óthin at break of day soliloquizes—he has dreamed of the advent into Valholl of a mighty king and that great preparations were made for his reception. But now, great din arises, and he asks Bragi, the god of Skaldic art, what it might be. No less joyful it sounds, Bragi thinks, than if Baldr himself were returning—Baldr whose fall was most fateful to the gods, and whose longed-for return to Valholl would be for them a matter of the greatest rejoicing![1] But Óthin, better acquainted with Fate, recognizes King Eric from afar and bids two of the heroes of the olden times rise up and welcome him: *ragnarok,* the Doom of the Gods, is approaching, and heroes such as Eric will be needed for the impending battle with the monsters of destruction. Eric draws near; and with him enter into Valholl no less than five kings slain in battle—worthy retinue for his apotheosis![2]

The form of the poem is quite irregular—*málaháttr* followed by loosely built *lióthaháttr* stanzas. Though a skaldic effort, it is notably simple in style, and almost without kennings.

Old Norse Poems

ÓTHIN

1 "What dreams be these, now? Methought that ere daybreak
I got Valholl ready to make room for warriors;
I waked the einheriar,[3] asked them to rise up,
to put straw on benches, and to rinse the beer-jugs;
and the valkyries, to deal wine out as though a warrior drew nigh.

2 "Lords from man-home[4] are to be looked for,
high-born and hardy, which my heart gladdens.

3 "What thunders, Bragi, as though thousands stirred,
     or whelming hosts?"

BRAGI

"Crack all boards of the benches as though Baldr were coming
     back to Óthin's beer-hall."

125

ÓTHIN

4 "Of witless words shalt beware, wise Bragi,
       for full well thou wotst:
    't is Eric this heralds, who to us is wending,
       the earl, into Óthin's hall.

5 "Sigmund and Sinfiotli, leave your seats, ye heroes,
       and go forth to greet the king!
    Bid him enter in, if Eric it be:
       him I have hopes to see."

SIGMUND

6 "Why of Eric, rather than of another?"

ÓTHIN

"Because in many a liege-land this lord hath warred
    and borne a bloody sword."

SIGMUND

7 "Why, then, didst rob him of victory,
since valiant thou thought'st him?"[5]

ÓTHIN

"No one knoweth—
looks the grey wolf (grimly)[6] toward
the gods' dwellings."

SIGMUND

8 "Hail to thee, Eric, here thou art
welcome!
  wise war-lord, in hall.
This fain would I know: who be
following thee
  of athelings, from the edge[7]-
fight?"

ERIC

9 "Kings five there are, them all I shall
name thee:
  am I the sixth myself."

Footnotes

1 Cf. *Baldr's Dreams*, 6, 7; *Voluspó*, 24 ff.

2 It is interesting to note that in that spirited Anglo-Saxon poem of the *Battle of Brunanburh*, fought not so many years before (937) and under similar circumstances, the bodies of five kings likewise lie on the battlefield (line 28).

3 The fallen warriors who are gathered by the valkyries into Óthin's hall; cf. *Vafthrúthnismól*, 41.

4 The earth.

5 The same reproach is hurled at Óthin by Loki, *Lokasenna*, 22:

"Hush thee, Óthin; not ever fairly
    didst allot men luck in battle.
Oft thou gavest, as give thou shouldst not,
    mastery to worser men."

6 Conjecture. Óthin's defense is that the best of (fallen) heroes — the *einheriar* — will be needed in the final battle with the Wolf, Fenrir (cf. *Voluspó*, 45 f.).

7 Pars *pro toto* for "sword."

Old Norse Poems

The Lay of Hákon
[Hákonarmól]
by Eyvind Finnsson Skáldaspillir

If the *Lay of Eric* was "made to order" by an unknown poet, as the eulogium of an unpopular, though brave, king, the *Lay of Hákon* is composed by the best-known of Norwegian skalds, unquestionably of his own accord, to commemorate his generally beloved leader. Hence the warmth of feeling, the note of personal loss, which pervades this splendid poem.

Hákon, surnamed the Good, a child of Harold Hairfair's old age, had been fostered by King Æthelstan of England, and thus brought up a Christian. After overthrowing his half brother Eric he tried to introduce the new faith, but met with stubborn opposition and had to desist in order to keep his throne. He is described as an ideal ruler for the times, handsome, generous, warlike though not aggressive, during whose reign of twenty-six years Norway enjoyed comparative peace and good harvests. He repelled several attempts of the sons of Eric to repossess themselves of the kingdom with the help of the Danes, but was wounded in a (victorious) battle against them on the island of Storth in southwest Norway (961) and died soon thereafter.

The poet Eyvind Finnsson was himself a distant relative of the king. We know that he lived in moderate circumstances and was a man of character. His (much-debated) epithet of *skáldaspillir* seems to mean "despoiler of skalds"; and if so, must have been given him by his enemies who readily fastened on the fact that his best works, *Hákonarmól* and *Háleygiatal* — the latter a long genealogical poem — are quite evidently patterned, the one after *Eiriksmól*, the other, after *Ynglingatal*, by the earlier poet, Thióthólf of Hvin.

If, notwithstanding this lack of original inspiration, the *Lay of Hákon* has been generally admired, then as well as now, this is due, not only to the genuine warmth and sincerity, but also to the superior artistry which makes it, all in all, perhaps the finest monument of its kind erected by Northern antiquity.

Central, and similar down to details, in both *Eiriksmól* and *Hákonarmól*, is the hero-king's advent in Valholl; but whereas the former does not change scene (and thus achieves greater unity) the latter, with richer content, shifts from earth to heaven and back again to earth as it ebbs in the poet's plaint over the loss of the peerless king. Also in style *Hákonarmól* shows more variety — consciously striven for. Thus, the straightforward and sober style of the narrative stanzas contrasts with the typically skaldic, baroque overloading of the battle-scene, clamorous with gorgeous and bizarre kennings, and that again with the highly charged dramatic force of the dialogues and the elegiac sorrow of the final dirge. The meter likewise shows a carefully considered correspondence to the style and theme—simple, impressive *lióthaháttr* for the epic-dramatic and lyric portions, against the martial tramp and blare of *málaháttr* descriptive of the carnage.

Eyvind had no doubt both a political and an apologetic aim with his poem: it was to be a counterblast to *Eiriksmól* and outdo it in splendor, but also to save the king's good heathen reputation. If Hákon at his entrance in Valholl is suspicious of Óthin's attitude and refuses to abandon his arms, he has abundant cause to fear the god's wrath—his abortive defection from the heathen cause. And the good reception accorded him because he had "protected" the heathen fanes which, in fact, he had been powerless to destroy, may not have been altogether convincing to his contemporaries.[1] Also the heathen trappings, the copious reminiscences from such arch heathen poems as *Voluspó* and *Hóvamól*, the interest in the king shown by the valkyries, the delegation to receive him composed of the gods Bragi and Hermóth—the same who was to fetch Baldr back from Hel[2]—all seem deliberately chosen to link the king with the old religion and to rehabilitate him in the eyes of his people.

The complete poem is found in Snorri Sturlason's History of the Norwegian Kings (*Heimskringla*), at the end of *Hákonarsaga gótha*. Portions of it are transmitted also in *Fagrskinna*.

Old Norse Poems

1. Gautatýr[3] sent forth Gondul and Skogul[4]
   to choose among kings' kinsmen:
   who of Yngvi's offspring[5] should with Óthin dwell,
   and wend with him to Valhöll.

2. They found Biorn's brother[6] his byrnie donning,
   under standard standing the stalwart leader—
   were darts uplifted and spearshafts lowered;
   up the strife then started.

3. Called on Hálogaland's[7] heroes and Northaland's swordsmen
   the Northmen's folkwarder, ere he fared to battle:
   a good host had he of henchmen from Norway—
   the Danes'-terror donned his bronze-helm.[8]

4. Threw down his war-weeds, thrust off his byrnie[9]
   the great-hearted lord, ere began the battle—
   laughed with his liege-men; his land would he shield now,[10]
   the gladsome hero 'neath gold-helm standing.

5. Cut then keenly the king's broadsword
   through foemen's war-weeds, as though water it sundered.[11]
   Clashed then spear-blades, cleft were war-shields;
   did ring-decked[12] war-swords rattle on helmets.

6   Were targes trodden by the Týr-of-shields,[13]
by the hard-footed hilt-blade, and heads eke of Northmen;
battle raged on the island,[14] athelings reddened
the shining shield-castles[15] with shedded life-blood.

7   Burned the wound-fires[16] in bloody gashes,
were the long-beards[17] lifted against the life of warriors—
the sea-of-wounds[18] surged high around the swords' edges,
ran the stream-of-arrows[18] on the strand of Storth-isle.

8   Reddened war-shields rang 'gainst each other,
did Skogul's-stormblasts[19] scar red targes;
billowed blood-waves in the blast-of-Óthin[20]—
was many a man's son mowed down in battle.

9   Sate[21] then the liege-lords with swords brandished,
with shields shattered and shredded byrnies:
not happy in their hearts was that host of men,
    and to Valholl wended their way.

10 Spoke then Gondul, on spearshaft leaning:
    "groweth now the gods' following,[22]
since Hákon hath been with host so goodly
    hidden home by holy gods."

11 Heard the war-lord what the valkyries spoke of,
        high-hearted, on horseback—
    wisely they bore them, sitting war-helmeted,
        and with shields them sheltering.

HÁKON said:

12 "Why didst Geirskogul,[23] grudge us victory?
    Yet worthy were we that the gods granted it."

SKOGUL said:

13 "'Tis owing to us that the issue was won
        and your foemen did flee.

14 Ride forth now shall we," said fierce Skogul,
        "to the green homes of the godheads,—
    there to tell Óthin that the atheling will now
        come to see him himself."

15 "Hermóth and Bragi!" called out Hróptatýr:[24]
        "Go ye to greet the hero;
    for a king cometh who hath keenly foughten,
        to our halls hither."

16 Said the war-worker, wending from battle—
        was his byrnie all bloody:
    "Angry-minded Óthin meseemeth.
        Be we heedful of his hate!"

17 "All einheriar shall swear oaths to thee:
      share thou the Æsir's ale,
   thou enemy-of-earls!25 Here within hast thou
      brethren eight," said Bragi.

18 "Our gear of war," said the goodly king,
      "we mean to keep in our might.
   helmet and hauberk one should heed right well:
      'tis good to guard one's spear."26

19 Then was it seen how that sea-king had
      upheld the holy altars,
   since Hákon all did hail with welcome,
      both gods and heavenly hosts.

20 On a good day is born that great-souled lord
      who hath a heart like his;
   aye will his times be told of on earth,
      and men will speak of his might.27

21 Unfettered will fare the Fenriswolf,
      and fall on the fields of men,
   ere that there cometh a kingly lord
      as good, to stand in his stead.28

22 Cattle die and kinsmen die,29
      land and lieges are whelmed;
   since Hákon to the heathen gods fared
      many a host is harried.30

Old Norse Poems

Footnotes

<u>1</u> Though we may in this stanza also see a reflection on his successors who ravaged the sanctuaries and hid the gold.

<u>2</u> Cf. *Baldr's Dreams*.

<u>3</u> "The God of the Gauts." *i.e.*, Óthin.

<u>4</u> Valkyries.

<u>5</u> Yngvi generally stands for Freyr in his capacity of progenitor of the Swedish kings. Here, however, he stands for Óthin, the progenitor of the royal race of Norway.

<u>6</u> Hákon. Biorn was one of the many sons of Harold Fairhair.

<u>7</u> Cf. *Haraldskvæthi*, note 37. Horthaland is here substituted for the Rogaland of the text. It is directly south of the latter.

<u>8</u> The change to the golden helmet (in the next stanza) has been referred to an episode of the battle as told by Snorri: "Hákon was more easily recognized than other men, and his helmet glittered when the sun shone on it. He always was in the thick of the fray. Then Eyvind Finnsson (our poet) drew a hood over it. Whereupon Eyvind skreya (one of the enemy) cried out: 'Is the king of Norway hiding now, or has he fled—else where is his golden helmet?' The king shouted: 'Come forward hither if you would find the King of Norway,' and in the ensuing hand-to-hand fight cleft his skull with his sword."

<u>9</u> This was not uncommon with fierce warriors, in the heat of battle.

10 Viz., against the sons of Eric.

11 At his departure from England, his foster father, King Æthelstan, gave him the sword Quernbiter with which Hákon is said to have cut a millstone in two.

12 Swords frequently had rings on the hilt, for carrying.

13 The following stanzas are examples of Skaldic style overloaded with kennings; though not as complicated and disjointed as was believed until recently. The Týr (god)-of-shields (or rings) is a kenning for "warrior." In ordinary language the first part of the stanza says that the shields and the heads of Northmen were trodden (hewed) by the hardened steel of the king (Kock).

14 Viz., of Storth.

15 The serried shields thrown about the king.

16 Kenning for "sword."

17 Kenning for "battle-axe."

18 Kenning for "blood."

19 *I.e.*, the mutual attacks. The difficulties, both of interpretation and translation, are considerable.

20 Kenning for "battle."

21 Viz., dying.

22 Cf. *Eiriksmól*, 7, note, for the conception implied.

23 *I.e.,* Spear-Skogul.

24 "God of gods," *i.e.,* Óthin.

25 "Hero."

26 Cf. *Hovamól,* 1. I follow Kock's suggestion.

27 There is reference here, probably, to his favor with the gods, manifest in good harvests and general prosperity.

28 Cf. *Voluspó* 36, 54: not till the end of the world will a better ruler come.

29 Patently, a reminiscence of the famous stanzas 77, 78 of *Hóvamól.*

30 This is, very likely, an allusion to the lawless times that followed the reign of Hákon.

Lee M. Hollander

Old Norse Poems

The Song of the Valkyries
[Darraðarljóð]

"ON Good Friday it happened in Caithness[1] that a man called Dorroth went out of doors. He saw twelve persons ride toward a (stone) hut. There they were lost to his sight. When he came up to the hut and looked through a chink in the wall he saw that some women were inside and had set up a web. Heads of men served as weights, men's entrails formed the woof and weft, a sword did as a weaver's reed, and arrows as the rods. They sang this song: (follows the *Song of the Valkyries*). Then they tore the web down and into pieces, and each one held on to what she had in her hands. Dorroth right the opening and went home; but the women mounted their horses and rode away — six to the south and six to the north."

Thus the *Niáls saga* (Chapter 157), whose narrative is our sole source for one of the most striking poems of Norse antiquity. Down to Walter Scott's days it was recited in the Norn tongue by the inhabitants of North Ronaldsha (*Rinansey*), the northernmost of the Orkney Islands.[2]

As we have it, the lay is darkly prophetic of the outcome of the great battle of Clontarf (1014) in which some of the actors in the saga took part on the side of the Viking leaders, Sigtrygg Silkbeard, King of Dublin, and the Orkney earl, Sigurth Hlothversson, who were arrayed against the famous King Brian Borumha of Leinster; but contrary to its prophecy, history—and the saga, too—tells us that it was the Leinster king who won the victory, though he paid for it with his life, and that the invaders were driven off, leaving Earl Sigurth on the field. To account for this contradiction, some scholars have surmised that the lay originally referred to some other battle. Against this it may be urged that at any rate Sigurth's fall is foretold, in stanza 7. Also, it is just possible that the Irish themselves are meant as the dwellers on the outer nesses in their own land (*ibid.*) and that the valkyries are chanting their magic song to safeguard only their favorite, the young King Sigtrygg, weaving for him the "web of war"—much as the giant maidens in the *Quern Song* "grind out" the fate of their captor, King Fróthi.

As to the supposed transmitter of the lay, Dorroth, it seems that his name was supplied, either from the kenning in stanza 4, the "web-of-darts," *i.e.*, "battle" (*vefr darratha(r)*) or, even more probably, from the (unauthentic and inappropriate) current title of the lay, *Darratha(r)lióth* or *Lay of the Darts* which was misunderstood as *Dorroth's Lay*.

Old Norse Poems

Few lays in Old Norse compare with the *Song of the Valkyries* in somber power and dark magnificence. Thoroughly in harmony with the great carnage presaged is the gruesome picture of the loom; and terribly splendid the vision of the red dawn with its cloud-rack incarnadined by the blood of warriors, into which the battle maidens issue forth, riding on wild horses to join the fray.

The lay—which is in regular *fornyrthislag*—is handed down in the four main MSS of the *Niáls saga*, dating from the fourteenth to the seventeenth century, but seems incomplete, for all that, and is in poor shape.[3] In this case it is not altogether unlikely that the author was an inhabitant of the Northern Isles. At any rate it is well to remember that still another poetic prophecy—a genre more Celtic than Germanic in inspiration—viz., the *Quern Song*, right memories in these localities where Norse and Celtic blended most intimately.

1   Widely is flung, warning of slaughter,
    the weaver's-beam's-web:[4] 't is wet with blood;
    is spread now, grey, the spear-thing[5] before,
    the woof-of-the-warriors[4] which valkyries fill
    with the red-warp-of- Randvér's-banesman.[6]

2   Is this web woven and wound of entrails,
    and heavy weighted with heads of slain;
    are blood-bespattered spears the treadles,
    iron-bound the beams, the battens,[7] arrows:
    let us weave with our swords this web of victory!

3   Goes Hild to weave, and Hiorthrimul,
    Sangrith and Svipul,[8] with swords brandished:
    shields will be shattered, shafts will be splintered,
    will the hound-of-helmets[9] the hauberks bite.

4   Wind we, wind we the-web-of-darts,
    and follow the atheling after to war!
    Will men behold shields hewn and bloody
    where Gunn and Gondul[8] have guarded the thane.

5   Wind we, wind we such web-of-darts
    as the young war-worker waged afore-time![10]
    Forth shall we fare where the fray is thickest,
    where friends and fellows 'gainst foemen battle!

Old Norse Poems

6 Wind we, wind we   the web-of-darts
where float the flags   of unflinching men!
Let not the liege's   life be taken:
valkyries award   the weird of battle.[11]

7 Will seafaring men   hold sway over lands,
who erstwhile dwelled   on outer nesses;
is doomed to die   a doughty king,[12]
lies slain an earl   by swords e'en now

8 Will Irish men eke   much ill abide:
't will not ever after   be out of men's minds.
Now the web is woven,   and weapons reddened—
in all lands will be heard   the heroes' fall.

9 Now awful is it   to be without,
as blood-red rack   races overhead;
is the welkin gory   with warriors' blood
as we valkyries   war-songs chanted.

10 Well have we chanted   charms full many
about the king's son: may it bode him well!
Let him learn them   who listens to us,
and speak these spells   to spearmen after.[13]

11 Start we swiftly   with steeds unsaddled—
hence to battle   with brandished swords!

145

Footnotes

<u>1</u> The northeastern-most district of Scotland.

<u>2</u> The poem had struck the imagination of Thomas Gray, who in 1768 made a free version of it which he entitled *The Fatal Sisters*. In 1814, when Scott was on his voyage among the northern islands of Great Britain, he heard a gentleman tell that when some remnants of the Norse were yet spoken there, a clergyman had carried thither Gray's version, then newly published, and had read it to some old people as referring to the ancient history of the islands. But as soon as he had proceeded a little way they exclaimed they knew it well in the original and had often sung it. They called it "The Enchantress" (Lockhart, *Memoirs of the Life of Sir Walter Scott*, IV, 81. See also *The Pirate*, Note c).

<u>3</u> In order not to overload the footnotes I have tacitly essayed an approximation in the translation of the first and second stanzas as well as in numerous other doubtful passages.

<u>4</u> Kenning for "battle." The same conception, growing out of the interweaving of darts and arrows in the air, is found in the Anglo-Saxon *wīgspēda gewiofu*, "the web of battle-luck" (*Bēowulf* 697). The two parts of this difficult stanza are parallel: a web is set up, the "web-of-battle," which is all stained with blood.

<u>5</u> Another kenning for "battle." (Thing = "meeting.")

<u>6</u> The whole line, probably, a kenning for "blood." Randvér's banesman was Bikki, the evil counselor of Iormunrekk (cf. *Guthrúnarhvot*, Prose, and note 8), in whom—as in Gizur (*Battle of the Huns*)—we may detect Óthin, the instigator of strife between men. "Fill" is here, probably, used in the sense of

completing the web with woof and weft. But it might also mean "to saturate" and so, "to color."

7 The batten is the instrument used to beat home the yarn. Much also in this stanza is doubtful.

8 The names of valkyries.

9 Kenning for "battle-axe."

10 Granting that "the web-of-darts" is a kenning for "battle" (from the cloud, or web, of missiles flying overhead), the meaning of this uncertain line is that the valkyries are urging each other on to "weave" another such victorious battle as the young king (Sigtrygg) had before. Cf. Eiríkr Magnússon, *Old-lore Miscellany of Orkney* III, 92.

11 It is for the valkyries to decide the fate of battle and to choose the slain: they have no need of his life.

12 *I.e.,* King Brian, who was set upon at the very end of the battle. The earl, Sigurth Hlothversson, had fallen earlier.

13 A hint to the listener outside.

Lee M. Hollander

Old Norse Poems

The Curse of Busla
[Buslubœn]

The mysterious power of the word, whether for prayer, benediction or malediction, has been felt at all times. And at all times, both good wishes and imprecations have been apt to clothe themselves in some kind of metric-rhythmic form for greater expressiveness and impressiveness, for enhancing their magic power. And no sooner is the "formula" fixed than the need is felt to perpetuate the passing sound of words of such power and value by symbols through which their effect may be multiplied, and even conveyed to some distance in time and space. In the Germanic North the runes — alphabetic signs which were adopted, it seems, from some Mediterranean alphabet, say, about the beginning of our era[1] — served this purpose, especially when verbal curses had failed.[2] They were scratched ("written") on stone and wood and bone and metal, on weapons, clothing, implements of all kinds to be used by him in whose favor, or against whom, the magic was to take effect.

Old High German and Anglo-Saxon literature offers us a wealth of examples of healing, or defensive, magic formulae — some of them of literary value, like the Merseburg Incantations; but for extended instances of offensive magic we must go to Old Norse literature. The Eddic poems abound with magic of all sorts. As illustrations of "offensive" magic we may point out the "classic" curses of Skírnir and of Sigrún, and the shorter malisons of *Lokasenna, Fiólsvinnsmól, Atlamól*.[3] A monument wholly devoted to the purpose of wishing ill "on" some one, and perhaps the most instructive of its kind in literature, though admittedly on a lower plane in æsthetic value than those mentioned, is the *Buslubœn* of the *Bósa saga*, a Romantic fornaldar saga (legendary tale) of the thirteenth century. Neither is the curse, as a whole, much older; witness certain phrases and views; which, however, does not preclude some portions breathing rank age-old heathendom. It will be noted, by the way, that the last stanza, containing the fiercest rune-magic, does not seem to belong here originally; for whereas all the others contain some proviso, the effectiveness of this curse is dependent, not on King Hring complying with Busla's demands, but on his not solving the runic riddle. Very likely, the monument is fragmentary, whether through the pretended squeamishness of the clerical scribe or, as seems more likely, through his not remembering more.

The saga tells how, impelled by untoward circumstances, young Herrauth and his companion at arms, Bósi, fight a pitched battle with Herrauth's father, King Hring. They are subdued and bound, to be put to death on the morrow; but old Busla, Bósi's fostermother, a hag most experienced in witchcraft, approaches the king at night "and began that curse which is since called Busla's Curse. It has become famous. In it are many turns which are bad for Christians to have in their mouths. And this is the beginning of it:"

1   "Here liest thou, Hring, Lord of the Gauts,[4]
    the most headstrong of human kind—
    minded, to-morrow to murther thy son:
    will this foul deed be told far and wide.

2   "Hear thou Busla's songs—[5] 't will be sung full soon;
    so that it be heard the whole world about—
    harmful to him who heareth it,
    but fellest for him whom fain I would curse.

3   "May wights be wildered, and wonders happen,
    may cliffs be shattered and the world shaken,
    may the weather worsen, and wonders happen,
    but thou, King Hring, forgive Herrauth,
       and eke to Bósi no ill threaten.

4   "O'er thy chest such charms now chant I shall[6]
    that evil asps shall eat thy heart,
    that thy ears henceforth shall hear no more,
    and thy seeing eyes leave their sockets,
       but thou with Bósi wilt bear, hereafter,
       nor harbor hate against Herrauth, either.

Old Norse Poems

5 "If boat thou sailest, shall burst the ropes,
   if boat thou steerest, shall break the tholepins[7]—
   shall the sail-cloth be slit and sag downward,
   and all the tackle be torn asunder,
      but thou harbor no hate against Herrauth,
   and but thou with Bósi will bear hereafter.

6 "Shall the reins ravel when thou ridest forth,
   shall horses go halt, and nags be hamstrung[8]—
   shall both highways and bridle-paths
   take thee where trolls may tear thee straightway,
      but thou with Bósi wilt bear hereafter,
   nor harbor hate against Herrauth, either.

7 "May thy bed be for thee like burning straw,
   thy high-seat unsteady like heaving sea-wave.
   Yet woe awaits thee much worse by far:
   if with maid thou meanest a man's joy to have,
   shalt lose thy way then:[9] doest wish to hear
   more?"

(The king attempts to silence her and to rise, but finds himself charmed fast to his bed and unable to wake his attendants. As he is still unwilling to give in, Busla chants the second part of her curse:)

8   "Shall trolls and elves and tricking witches,
    shall dwarfs and etins burn down thy mead-hall—
    shall thurses hate thee and horses ride thee,[9]
    shall all straws stick thee,[10] all storms stun thee:
    and woe worth thee but my will thou doest!"

(Then the king is ready to pardon his son Herrauth, but to declare Bósi outlaw.) Then started she to chant what is called *Syrpuvers* (*i.e.*, "the Verses of Syrpa"), in which is the strongest magic, so that it is not permitted to chant them after nightfall; and toward the end it goes like this:

9   Come here six fellows: say thou their names:
    I shall show them to thee unshackled all.
    But thou get them guessed as good meseemeth,
    shall ravening hounds rive thee to pieces,
    and thy soul sink to hell-fire!"[11]

(Then, after the king's swearing an oath that he will do her bidding, she "takes the curse off.")

Footnotes

1 The theory long accepted, that they originated through some adaptation of a Greek or Latin alphabet by the Goths along the Black Sea has recently been challenged with some force, and an earlier origin from Etruscan or Thracian script suggested.

2 Cf. *Skírnismól*, 38, note.

3 *Skírnismól, Helgakvitha Hundingsbana*, II, 30-33; *Lokasenna*, 65; *Fiolsvinnsmól*, 45; *Atlamól*, 30. Cf. also *Hervararkvitha*, 12, 21.

4 The inhabitants of Gautland, the present Swedish province of Gotland.

5 Literally, "prayer"; but the incantation is meant, of course.

6 The translation of the line is doubtful.

7 In Germanic antiquity, vessels were steered, not with a rudder, but with an extra oar on the "starboard," *i.e.*, the steering side. Oars were held by thongs to the tholepins. Cf. *Haraldskvæthi*, 17; *Atlamól*, 34.

8 Literally, "become weak."

9 To be understood in *malam partem*.

10 Proverbial for all things "going against one."

__11__ There follow these runic signs:

[runic signs]

As a solution, Uhland (*Schriften,* VI, 248) suggested that with the letters of the first group of runes successively placed before the five others, the six words (or "fellows," as the text has it) resulting would be *ristill* "plowshare," *aistill* "testicle," *thistill* "thistle," *kistill* "box," *mistill* "mistletoe," *vistill* "?" — words whose sense in *malam partem* is still partly discernible.

Old Norse Poems

The Oath of Truce
[Tryggthamól]

PRIMITIVE law, based as it is on the profoundest ethical convictions and sentiments of the race, has many elements in common with poetry. Especially is this the case when the law seeks to instance, or motivate, or elaborate, sanctions or punishments. Thus we find embedded in the Icelandic laws, following a treatment of weregild or composition for manslaughter, etc., a formula of peace[1] which both in form and spirit is essentially poetic. Indeed, when passion infuses itself—as where a mighty curse is called down on the violator of these oaths—heights of truly great poetry are reached: for the benefit of both witnesses and the interested parties, the abstract "everywhere" in which outlawry will be visited on him is translated into concrete images which pass before the mind's eye in an artless series of vivid impressions from the life of man, the boundless earth, the sky and the sea.

Like other, similar, snatches in the laws, the *Tryggthamól* are most instructive to the student of Old Germanic poetry in showing a more primitive stage of alliterative verse than that seen in epic or lay. There is as yet no regularity of metrical line, though a few normal long-lines do occur;[2] far less, any strophic structure. Still, alliteration has here its basic function of marking and reinforcing the natural stress, variation (parallelism) shows the instinctive fondness of the race for dwelling on favorite objects or conceptions; and the occasionally magnificent rhythm anticipates the effects of the more regular art practice to come. In other words, there are here, as in embryo, all the peculiar and stirring elements of Old Germanic poetry.

It is reasonable to suppose that these oaths are age-old and were brought over to Iceland from the common home in Norway.[3] Certainly the groundstock is heathen; the references to Christian belief and practices are but natural later accretions.

The version here translated is that of the so-called *Konungabók* or "Kings' Book" MS of the *Grágás*,[4] a twelfth-century compilation of Icelandic laws. A shorter version exists also in the so-called *Statharhólsbók,* or "Book of Statharhól Bishopric" MS of the *Grágás*. Besides, we have versions with important divergences in the seventy-second chapter of the *Grettis saga* and the thirty-third chapter of the *Heitharvíga saga*.

Old Norse Poems

There has been strife between N. N. and N. N.; but now peace has been made between them,
>and amends made
>as the domesmen deemed
>and the judges judged
>and the awarders weighed.
>Hath the offer been taken
>as even-handed,
>with full fees
>and forth-paid ounces,5
>to them handseled
>who were to have them.

Ye shall henceforth be men
>at peace and pledged
>at ale and eating,
>at thing and at folk-meet,
>at kirk-going
>and in king's hall;

and wherever men gather together, there shall ye be so agreed as though this matter had never come between you. Ye shall share
>both steel and steaks
>and all the things
>that are betwixt you,
>like friends7 and not like foes.

And if, later, strife arise between you twain and things be not in good case, then shall it
>be settled by fees,
>but no swords reddened.

But that one of you
    who is traitor to this truce
    and goes against word given,
he shall be
    as ill outlaw
    hunted and hated,
    so far as men ever
    an outlaw hunt,
    as Christian folk
    visit churches,
    as Heathen folk
    have hallowed shrines,
    as fire doth flame
    and earth is green,—
    as babe calleth mother,
    and mother suckles child,
    as folks kindle fire,
    ships sail the sea,
    and shields are borne,
    as the sun shineth,
    snow drifteth,
    Finn glideth,[8]
    fir-tree groweth,
    as falcon flie'th
    on a fair summer-day[9]
    with a brisk-blowing breeze
    under both his wings,
    as the sky arches
    and earth is tilled,
    wind doth howl,
    waters flow seaward,
    and seed is sown.

Old Norse Poems

He shall shun
churches and churched ones,
God's house and men's homes—
every abode
but hell only.

Now hold ye both this book[10] on which lies also the money
which N. N. offers as redress for himself and his heir.
 born or unborn,
 begotten or unbegotten,
 named or unnamed.

N. N. accepts this composition, and N. N. swears an
everlasting peace. It is to hold
 the while earth lasteth,
 and live on it men.
Now, then, are N. N. and N. N.
 agreed and at one,
 where'er they may meet—
 on shore or on water,
 on ship or on snow-shoe,
 on high sea or on horseback,
 to share in the rowing
 or in baling out,
 on bench or on deck,
 if need there be,
 at one with each other
 as is father with son
 or son with father,
 in all their dealings.

Now N. N. and N. N. shall clasp hands: hold ye well this truce, to the liking of Christ and of all the men who have now heard this oath of peace.

    May he have God's grace
    who holds this truce,
    but his wrath, who rives
    rightful truce—
    his grace, he who holds it!
Be ye now happy and at peace!
    Witnesses be we
    who about you stand!

Footnotes

[1] It is there called Tryggthamól or "Oaths of Peace." They are to be repeated, after the judge or umpire, by both parties to the suit.

[2] I have therefore printed the whole in half-lines.

[3] A few lines of the beginning, found in the fragmentary MS of the *Older Gulathingslóg* or "Laws of the Gula (legal) district" of Norway prove it.

[4] Literally. "Grey Goose" — from the MS covers of grey fur.

Old Norse Poems

5 *I.e.*, of silver.

6 In the original: "knife and meat-piece."

7 In the original: "like kinsmen."the closest bond between persons being that of the clan.

8 Viz., on skis.

9 Which, it will be remembered, in the Northland lasts most of the twenty-four hours.

10 The Bible, of course.

Lee M. Hollander

Old Norse Poems

The Riddles of King Heithrek,
[Heithreksgátur]

RIDDLES belong to the popular amusements of probably all races endowed with sufficient intellectual vivacity and reflective power to discover analogies. Yet but few collections of them possess literary value, or even originality, of any sort.

As is so frequently the case, our Old Norse representative of this genre does show originality, both in subject and treatment. Moreover, though the collection is restricted in extent, and cannot, as a whole, lay claim to great esthetic merit, it is of exceeding interest through its revealing autochthonous, naïve folk-thought. Most of its riddles are based on specifically North Scandinavian, or at least, Northern, environment, beliefs, and conceptions; and are presented in the patterns evolved in the same region—the greater part in more or less regular *fornyrthislag* and *lióthaháttr* stanzas. Again, the plastic genius of the North is evident in the many sharply observed traits of nature, whose outlines are not blurred by too great subtlety. Compared with them, the only other notable extant

Old Germanic collection, viz., the Anglo-Saxon riddles of the Exeter Book, will at once be seen to have all the earmarks of sophistication. And, notwithstanding the several distinct levels of style, ranging from the homespun manner of such riddles as the seventh, twelfth, sixteenth, and twenty-eighth, to the elaborate skaldic diction, with involved kennings, of a few others, these Northern riddles nowhere smack of "learning."

Intrinsically, the collection has nothing to do with the *Hervarar saga* in which it occurs, but has been rather skillfully connected with it by means of the widespread folklore motif of a king or giant allowing some one in his power to ransom himself, or attain the sought object, by guessing or propounding riddles. With variations, it is used in Old Norse literature in such poems as *Vafthrúthnismól, Alvíssmól, Baldrs draumar, Fiolsvithsmól;* but, to be sure, for the ulterior purpose of inculcating the knowledge of mythical lore.

The translation here offered follows the arrangement of the *Hauksbók* MS—or rather, its derivatives—which is according to form, rather than to contents; which latter is the principle followed by the other main MS of the *Hervarar saga*.

According to the saga, Hervor has two sons by King Heithrek, Angantýr and Heithrek; of whom the latter inherits both the ruthlessness of his mother and the wisdom of his father. When king, he makes the vow "that, however much a man had wronged him, he should have the chance of trial by his councillors, and that he should go scotfree, if he could propound any riddle the king could not solve, or else lose his head." A certain thane of Heithrek's, Gestumblindi,[2] had incurred the wrath of the king. In his distress he sacrificed to Óthin. One night a man came to Gestumblindi, so like him that no one could tell them apart. They exchanged garments and the stranger went up to court as Gestumblindi and insisted on his right to free himself by propounding riddles to the king.

GESTUMBLINDI said:

1. "That would I have which I had yesterday;
      heed what I had:
   men's hamperer, word's hinderer,
      and speeder of speech.
   Aright read now this riddle, Heithrek!"

HEITHREK said:

"Good is thy riddle, Gestumblindi,
      and guessed it is:
give him ale! That hampers many a man's wits; by it, some become talkative, but other men's wits are mazed."

GESTUMBLINDI said:

2. "From home I hied me, and from home faring
      I saw a way of ways:
   was a way beneath and a way above,
      and ways there were on all sides.
   Aright guess now this riddle, Heithrek!"

HEITHREK said: ~

"Good is thy riddle, Gestumblindi,
    and guessed it is:
You went over a bridge, the river ran under it, the birds flew above your head and on either side of you—that was their way."

GESTUMBLINDI said:

3 "What drink was it I drank yesterday?
    'twas neither wine nor water,
neither mead nor ale, nor meat,3 either;
    yet went I thirstless thence.
Aright guess now this riddle, Heithrek!"

HEITHREK said:

"Good is thy riddle, Gestumblindi,
    and guessed it is.
You lay down in the shade where the dew had fallen on the grass, and this cooled your lips and quenched your thirst.

GESTUMBLINDI said:

4 "Harshly he clangs, on hard paths treading
    which he has fared before.
Two mouths⁴ he has, and mightily kisses,
    and on gold alone he goes.
Aright guess now this riddle, Heithrek!"

HEITHREK said:

"Good is thy riddle, Gestumblindi,
        and guessed it is:
that is the goldsmith's hammer with which gold is
beaten."

GESTUMBLINDI said:

5 "Who is the great one that glides o'er the earth,
    and swallows both waters and woods?
The wind he fears, but wights nowise,
    and seeks to harm the sun.
Aright guess now this riddle, Heithrek!"

HEITHREK said:

"Good is thy riddle, Gestumblindi,
        and guessed it is:
That is the fog. One cannot see the sun because of him, but he disappears when the wind blows, and men can do naught against him. He kills the light of the sun."

GESTUMBLINDI said:

6 "Who is the mighty one who o'er much has sway,
        the half of whom turns toward Hel?
He saves many men but slashes the earth,
        if fast with trusty friend.
Aright guess now this riddle, Heithrek!"

HEITHREK said:

"Good is thy riddle, Gestumblindi,
        and guessed it is:
That is the anchor, with a stout and strong rope. It guards many a ship. It grips the earth with one fluke which thus turns Hel-ward. Many a man has been saved by it."

GESTUMBLINDI said:

7 "On high fells what lives? What falls in deep dales?
Without air what lives? What is not ever silent?
Aright guess now this riddle, Heithrek!"

HEITHREK said:

"Good is thy riddle, Gestumblindi,
 and guessed it is:
the raven always lives on high fells, the dew always
falls in deep dales, the fish live without air, and the
roaring waterfall is never silent."

GESTUMBLINDI said:

8 "What marvel is it which without I saw,
 before Delling's-door,5
with his head ever Hel-ward turning,
 with his feet seeking the sun.
Aright guess now this riddle, Heithrek!"

172

HEITHREK said:

"Good is thy riddle, Gestumblindi,
    and guessed it is:
That is the leek: its head₆ turns into the earth, but the leaves, upward."

GESTUMBLINDI said:

9 "What marvel is it which without I saw,
    before Delling's-door?
Were twain briskly, and breathless withal,
    boiling a wand-of-wounds.₇
Aright guess now this riddle, Heithrek!"

HEITHREK said:

"Good is thy riddle, Gestumblindi,
    and guessed it is:
they are the smith's bellows; they blow but have no breath."

GESTUMBLINDI said:

10 "What marvel is it which without I saw,
    before Delling's-door?
The white fliers on the flagstones bounded.
    but the swart ones sank in the sand.
Aright guess now this riddle, Heithrek!"

HEITHREK said:

"Good is thy riddle, Gestumblindi,
    and guessed it is:
they are hail and rain; because the hail beats on the flags, but the rain drops sink in the sand and go into the ground."[8]

GESTUMBLINDI said:

11 "What marvel is it which without I saw,
    before Delling's-door?
A black boar saw I bask in the mud,
    yet no bristles stood on his back.
Aright guess now this riddle, Heithrek!"

Heithrek said:

"Good is thy riddle, Gestumblindi,
    and guessed it is:
that is the dung-beetle."

Gestumblindi said:

12 "What marvel is it which without I saw,
        before Delling's-door?
Ten tongues has it, has twenty eyes
and forty feet, slowly fares that wight.
Aright guess now this riddle, Heithrek!"

Heithrek said:

"Good is thy riddle, Gestumblindi,
    and guessed it is:
you saw a sow in the farmyard with nine shoats in her." Then the king had the sow killed, and nine pigs were found in her, just as Gestumblindi had said.

GESTUMBLINDI said:

13 "What marvel is it which without I saw,
        before Delling's-door?
    Upward it flies with eagle's voice,
        and hard grip its claws the helmet.9
    Aright guess now this riddle, Heithrek!"

HEITHREK said:

"Good is thy riddle, Gestumblindi,
    and guessed it is:
that is the arrow."

GESTUMBLINDI said:

14 "What marvel is it which without I saw,
        before Delling's-door?
    Eight feet it has and four eyes,
        and its knees are above its belly.
    Aright guess now this riddle, Heithrek!"

HEITHREK said:

"Good is thy riddle, Gestumblindi,
 and guessed it is:
it is the spider."

GESTUMBLINDI said:

15 "What marvel is it which without I saw,
        before Delling's-door?
    It lights for men, and swallows up lights,10
        and wolves seek ever to win it.
    Aright guess now this riddle, Heithrek!"

HEITHREK said:

"Good is thy riddle, Gestumblindi,
 and guessed it is:
that is the Sun. He lights all the world and shines on all men; but there are two wolves, hight Skalli and Hatti, one of whom goes before, and the other follows, the sun."[11]

GESTUMBLINDI said:

16 "What marvel is it which without I saw,
      before Delling's-door?
   Harder than horn, blacker than Hel,[12]
   whiter than shell of egg,[13] straighter than shaft of spear.
   Aright guess now this riddle, Heithrek!"

HEITHREK said:

"Good is thy riddle, Gestumblindi,
      and guessed it is:
that is obsidian, with the sun shining on it."

GESTUMBLINDI said:

17 "Two brides did bear, white-blond their locks,
   and house-maids were they— ale-casks homeward;
   were they not shaped by hand nor by hammers wrought;
   yet upright[14] sate he on the isles, who made them.
   Aright guess now this riddle, Heithrek!"

HEITHREK said:

"Good is thy riddle, Gestumblindi,
> and guessed it is:
you saw two female swans going to their nests to
lay their eggs. Their shells are neither hand-made
nor wrought by hammers; but the he-swan sits out
on the islands, he that gat their eggs with them."

GESTUMBLINDI said:

18   "Who be the women on wilding fell?
> One bears a babe by the other,
and maid by maid a man-child begets,
> yet man has not touched these maids.
Aright guess now this riddle, Heithrek!"

HEITHREK said:

"Good is thy riddle, Gestumblindi,
> and guessed it is:
they are two angelica stalks standing together, with
a shoot[15] coming up between them."

GESTUMBLINDI said:

19 "Who be the women who, weaponless,
         for their king kill each other?
    Every day the dark ones shield him,
         but the fair ones aye go forth.16
    Aright guess now this riddle, Heithrek!"

HEITHREK said:

"Good is thy riddle, Gestumblindi,
     and guessed it is:
That is the game of *hneftafl*: weaponless, the
figures slay each other for the sake of their king.
The red ones17 are his followers.18

GESTUMBLINDI said:

20 "Who be the playmates that pass over the lands,
         seeming fair19 to their father?
    A white shield they show in winter,
         and a swart one in summer.
    Aright guess now this riddle, Heithrek!"

HEITHREK said:

"Good is thy riddle, Gestumblindi,
    and guessed it is:
they are the ptarmigans. They are white in winter and black in summer."

GESTUMBLINDI said:

21 "Who be the sisters that sorrowing fare,
        seeming fair to their father?
    Many a man their might hath known—
        and thus they live their lives.
    Aright guess now this riddle, Heithrek!"

HEITHREK said:

"Good is thy riddle, Gestumblindi,
    and guessed it is:
They are the billows. They are called the maids of Ægir." [20]

GESTUMBLINDI said:

22 "Who be the maids that fare, many together,
   seeming fair to their father?
   Whitish hair have the white-hooded ones,
   and no man is with the maids.
   Aright guess now this riddle, Heithrek!"

HEITHREK said:

"Good is thy riddle, Gestumblindi,
   and guessed it is:
but these are the waves, as before."

GESTUMBLINDI said:

23 "Who be the widows that band all together,
   seeming fair to their father?
   They are seldom kind to sailor-folk,
   and are wide awake in the wind.
   Aright guess now this riddle, Heithrek!"

HEITHREK said:

"Good is thy riddle, Gestumblindi,
>and guessed it is:
they are Ægir's widows. Thus are called the breakers."

GESTUMBLINDI said:

24 "Who be the women that wade in the surf
>and fare along the firths?
A hard bed have the white-hooded ones,
>and quiet are they in calm.
Aright guess now this riddle, Heithrek!"

HEITHREK said:

"Good is thy riddle, Gestumblindi,
>and guessed it is:
they are the billows—their beds are skerries and shingle, and they become somewhat sluggish in calm weather."

GESTUMBLINDI said:

25 "I saw traveling a soil's-earth-dweller,[21]
　　　a corpse sate on a corpse;
one blind rode a blind thing to the billows'-road,[22]
　　　and no life was in the nag.
Aright guess now this riddle, Heithrek!"

HEITHREK said:

"Good is thy riddle, Gestumblindi,
　　　and guessed it is:
you came to a river, and an ice-floe floated down it. On the floe lay a dead horse, and on the horse, a dead snake; so that one blind thing rode another blind thing."

GESTUMBLINDI said:

26 "What creature kills the cattle men have,
　　　and is iron-clad, without?
Eight horns it has, but head it has none,
　　　and runs when run it may.
Aright guess now this riddle, Heithrek!"

Old Norse Poems

HEITHREK said:

"Good is thy riddle, Gestumblindi,
    and guessed it is:
that is the *húnn*₂₃ on the checkerboard. It shares its
name with the bear, and it runs as soon as it is
overthrown."

GESTUMBLINDI said:

27 "What beast is it which brave men shelters?
It has a bloody back and wards off blows,
goes against spears, life-giving to some.
Against lords' left hand it lays its body.
Aright guess now this riddle, Heithrek!"

HEITHREK said:

"Good is thy riddle, Gestumblindi,
    and guessed it is:
that is the shield. It often becomes bloody in battle,
shielding those men who are handy with it."

185

GESTUMBLINDI said:

28   "Greatly had grown   a goose with big neb,
     had brought timber together, for goslings eager.
     Gave shelter to her   the sheaves'- bite-swords;24
     but above it lay the drink's-   dinful-rockcave,25
     Aright guess now   this riddle, Heithrek!"

HEITHREK said:

"Good is thy riddle, Gestumblindi,
        and guessed it is:
that is a duck which had built her nest between the
jaws of an ox, with the skull roofing above it."

GESTUMBLINDI said:

29   "Four do hang   and four do gang;
     two show the way,   two ward off dogs;
     one drags after,   most often dirty.
     Aright guess now   this riddle, Heithrek!"

Old Norse Poems

HEITHREK said:

"Good is thy riddle, Gestumblindi,
    and guessed it is:
that is a cow. She has four feet and four tits, two horns and two eyes, and her tail drags after her."

GESTUMBLINDI said:

30 "Who is the one that in the ashpit sleeps:
    and is only struck out of stone?
Neither father nor mother has the greedy fiend—
    there he wants to live his life.
Aright guess now this riddle, Heithrek!"

HEITHREK said:

"Good is thy riddle, Gestumblindi,
    and guessed it is:
that is the fire hidden in the hearth—it is struck out of flint."

GESTUMBLINDI said:

31 "A stallion stood bestriding a mare;
he put buttock 'neath belly and bobbed with his tail.
Draw it out and in, work at it long![26]
Aright guess now this riddle, Heithrek!"

HEITHREK said:

"Good is thy riddle, Gestumblindi,
    and guessed it is:
that horse is a piece of linen on the loom. His mare[27] is the weaver's reed, and up and down is the web to be shaken."[28]

GESTUMBLINDI said:

32 "Who be the thanes to the thing who ride?
    Sixteen are in that set.
Their liege-men send they over all the lands,
    to seek a place to settle.
Aright guess now this riddle, Heithrek!"

HEITHREK said:

"Good is thy riddle, Gestumblindi,
    and guessed it is:
they are Itrek and Andath[29] sitting on their checkerboard."

GESTUMBLINDI said:

33   "In the summer saw I, at sunset time,
a merry band at festive board;
the men did drink their mead in peace,
the while the mead-keg muttering stood.
Aright guess now this riddle, Heithrek!"

HEITHREK said:

"Good is thy riddle, Gestumblindi,
    and guessed it is:
that is a sow with her shoats. When the pigs suck her she grunts, while they keep quiet."

GESTUMBLINDI said:

34 "Maidens saw I which were much like dust;
    boulders served them as beds.
Are they swart and sallow in sunny weather,
    but the fairer, the fainter the light.
Aright guess now this riddle, Heithrek!"

HEITHREK said:

"Good is thy riddle, Gestumblindi,
    and guessed it is:
they are the gledes dying on the hearth."

GESTUMBLINDI said:

35 "On a sail I sate and saw dead men
who a blood-vein bore to the bark of a tree.30
Aright guess now this riddle, Heithrek!"

Old Norse Poems

HEITHREK said:

"Good is thy riddle, Gestumblindi,
 and guessed it is:
You sate on a wall and saw a falcon bear an eider duck to the cliff."

GESTUMBLINDI said:

36 "Who are the twain that on ten feet run?
three eyes they have, but only one tail.
Aright guess now this riddle, Heithrek!"

HEITHREK said:

"Good is thy riddle, Gestumblindi,
 and guessed it is:
that is Othin riding on Sleipnir."[31]

Then GESTUMBLINDI said:

37
"Guess one more riddle, since wiser thou seemest
than any other wight:[32]
what said Óthin in Baldr's ear
before he was borne to the fire?"[33]

The king answered:
"But wicked spells and wantonness
I ween that it was:
the words thou spakest no wight knoweth
but thou, ill and unclean wight."[34]

Then the king drew the sword Tyrfing and struck at Gestumblindi, but he changed himself into a hawk and flew out through the opening of the roof. The sword reached the hawk's tail, and that is why it now has a short tail, so heathen folk believe. But Óthin was now enraged at Heithrek, because he had struck at him. That same night the king was killed with Tyrfing (by thralls who sought revenge and their freedom).

Footnotes

1 More properly, they are to be solved by him.

2 *I.e.,* probably, *Gest hinn blindi,* "Gest the blind." This name, of course, properly belongs to Óthin himself.

3 In the sense of food in general.

4 In the Old Norse conception, the edges of a tool are called "mouths."

5 Possibly, a kenning for "dawn."

6 To be sure, only according to the Old Norse figure.

7 Kenning for "sword." It is "boiled," *i.e.,* the metal for it is melted by the bellows fanning the fire.

8 The solution would seem to be, rather, "melting hail."

9 The translation of this half-stanza is conjectural.

10 The text is uncertain; possibly, "water (fog) swallows it."

11 Cf. *Grímnismól,* 39; where they are called Skoll and Hati.

12 In the original: "than the raven." In Old Norse, volcanic glass—exceedingly common in Iceland—is called "raven-flint."

13 Or rather, than the inner membrane of the egg.

14 Or "eager." Both in *malam partem.*

15 In Old Norse this is called the "young" of the (Arch)angelica plant, much prized in Scandinavia as a delicacy.

16 I.e., to assail him.

17 I.e., the "dark ones."

18 This game was played on a checkerboard, with hemispherical figures of bone or glass, 12 against 13, the one party white, the other dark. The game turned on one main figure (hnefi) belonging to the dark party. The turns were decided by dice.

19 I follow Kock's suggestion for the translation of this formula.

20 The god of the sea. This and the following riddles closely resemble the one in *Baldr's Dreams*, 12, which there brings the dénouement. The billows "weep," casting their kerchief-corners to the sky—a figure easily interpreted.

21 Kenning for "worm" or "snake."

22 Kenning for "sea."

23 "She-bear." The game here referred to may have had some resemblance to "Hound and Hare." The figures are imagined as cattle killed by a bear. The *húnn* must have had the shape of a die since it is said to have eight corners (Old Norse horn may mean both "horn" and "corner"). One such figure was found in Iceland together with twenty-four others of which half were red and half, white. Bugge, *Norröne Skritter at Sagnhistorisk Indhold*, p. 358.

24 Literally: "the biting-blades-of-the-straw": Kenning for the "jaws" of an ox.

25 Kenning for "skull": the skull bones are compared to a passage, through stones, or a "cave," for drink.

26 Conjectural. The whole stanza of course *in malam partem*.

27 Obviously, the two are interchanged.

28 That is, the yarn of the woof must be alternately lifted up and pressed down with the help of the crosspiece. Bugge, *loc. cit.*, p. 360.

29 These are the names of the kings in a modification of chess.

30 This is a good example of the homonym riddle. Says Bugge, *ibid.*, p. 361: "The words that are to be guessed have two, altogether different, meanings in the original. Instead of these words, the riddle has expressions which may be said to have the same meaning as the one sense of the words to be guessed." Thus, "dead men" is put for *valr* "falcon," because this word may also signify "those fallen in battle." Instead of *æthr* "eider duck" is set *blóthshól* "vein," because *æthr* has also that sense. And apparently, according to Egilsson, *segl* "sail" is set for *væggr* "wall," which word may also mean "wedge" — the shape of the triangular sail. The last line has so far defied explanation.

31 Óthin's steed which has eight legs; cf. *Grímnismól*, 44. Óthin himself has but one eye, having pledged the other to Mimir; cf. *Voluspó*, 21. This riddle properly leads to the next, and the dénouement.

32 Prose in the original, but probably representing a half-stanza. Restored here after Bugge's suggestion.

33 The same, insoluble, question — and thus not really a riddle — is propounded in *Vafthrúthnismól*, 55.

34 This stanza, likewise, is in the best MSS resolved into prose. Cf. the similar situation at the end of *Grímnismól*.

Old Norse Poems

The SUN SONG
[SÓLARLIÓTH]

WITH THIS CURIOUS POEM we are in another world—that of medieval Christian thought, morality, symbols. Yet, strangely, there is in it far more of the old and heathen than would appear at first blush. Indeed, nothing shows more strikingly the saturation and penetration of the North with the traditional "heathen," alliterative art than that such an arch-Catholic poem as *Sólarlióth* is composed in one of the time-honored forms, *lióthaháttr* or "chant meter"[1]— the measure which is firmly associated with that arch-heathen collection, *Hóvamól*. Moreover, there is little doubt that the author consciously patterned his poem—more specially, the first part of it—on the general plan of that unique collection of saws in the Germanic spirit. The heathen tradition is seen no less clearly in numerous stylistic and phraseological reminiscences from the older collection; so that it would seem that the author, some pious Icelandic cleric of, say, the thirteenth century, was steeped in the gnomic lore of his forefathers before even conceiving his poem. Still further, there are certain similarities with *Hugsvinnsmól*,[2] the translation, (also in *lióthaháttr*, and possibly by the same person) of the *Dicta Catonis*, a Latin collection of wise saws in distichs which was very popular in the Middle Ages. Like the *Sun Song*, it is addressed by a father to his son. Neither is the substance of our poem, with its inculcation of Christian ethics, by parable and precept, of any great originality, familiar as that subject was through a multitudinous literature of homilies, visions, books of devotion. The great interest, aye, fascination, of the poem lies, rather, in the remarkable blending and interpenetration of all these elements to form something individually new which, once read, is not easily forgotten. It has been aptly called a Christian Eddic lay, a Christian *Hóvamól*; though it is hardly open to debate that, both as a whole and in its parts, it is greatly inferior to its prototype.

The beginning seems abrupt, suggesting the loss of some introductory stanza or stanzas, to conform with those of the conclusion (81-82). But for the rest, it appears now, thanks to the searching investigations, during recent years, of a number of scholars, that the poem forms a fairly comprehensible and reasonably logical whole; especially when bearing in mind the visionary character of the latter part and the nature of its literary sources. They serve to explain a certain general looseness of structure and a baffling incoherence of thought which has led some students to doubt the unity of the poem.

Old Norse Poems

As stated, the poem deals with the Christian way of life, by examples (1-24) and precepts (the seven Christian counsels, 25-32); but chiefly by impressive personal experience of death, and of life in the Beyond, the sight of the punishments and rewards meted out to sinner and saint (33-75). This scheme leaves as obscure in bearing (and detail) only stanzas 76-80.[3]

The name of the poem, revealed in 81, seems to have reference, not so much to the famous initial burthen of the central portion: "The sun I saw," as to the Sun as the well-known symbol of Christ.

We are dependent for our knowledge of the poem on Paper MSS of the seventeenth century which may all be referred to one and the same original.

Lee M. Hollander

1 Of life and goods did the grim warrior[4]
       rob men wrongfully;
   by the way which was watched by him,
       no quick wight ever came.

2 By himself (most often)[5] he ate alone,
       nor e'er bade men to his meals;
   till once, weary and weak of strength
       a wayfarer he welcomed.

3 Of meat and drink he[6] seemed much in need,
       and faint without food;
   now, frightened, he must fain trust him
       who ere had been hard of heart.

4 Gave he meat and drink to the drooping man,
       and whole-heartedly, withal;
   good fare he gave him, of God mindful,
       for well he wished the man.[7]

5 Up he got, on ill deeds bent,
       nor gratefully took what was given:
   his sin swelled,[8] he the sleeping man murdered
       who wise and wary was else.

Old Norse Poems

6   To Heavens' God for help he prayed
        when waking, wounded to death;
   but on him fell the heavy sin:
        who had dastardly done him to death.

7   Came holy angels from Heaven above,
        and swiftly seized his soul;
   A sinless life will it lead thereafter,
        aye with almighty God.

                * * *

8   Nor health nor wealth— though all go well with him[9]—
        may a man ever master;
   misfortune befalls him who feared it least:
        by himself, no one settles the issue.

9   Neither Unnar nor Sævaldi[10] would e'er have thought
        that fortune would fail them at last;
   naked they both were banished from men,[11]
        and ran as "wolves"[12] to the woods.

                * * *

10   The might of love hath brought many to grief:
         oft cometh woe of women:
     they grew evil though God almighty
         had created them clean.13

11   Sworn friends they were, Sváfath and Skart-
     hethin,
         nor would one be without the other;
     till by one woman bewitched they were:
         was she born to undo them both.

12   Listless of all, for love of the girl—
         of games and gatherings—
     no other thing could they think about,
         for love of the lily-white maid.

13   Were dreary for them the darksome nights,
         nor could they slumber or sleep;
     till out of that grief there grew up hate
         'twixt men who were friends before.

14   Of monstrous things, as is mostly the case,
         the outcome was seen full soon:
     on the holm they went14 for the winsome maid,
         and did each other to death.

* * *

Old Norse Poems

15   Let man beware of o'erweening pride—
        that have I seen in sooth;
    for away from God they wander all
        who keep them not clean of it.

16   Were mighty and rich Ráthný and Vébothi,[15]
        and deemed they did but good;
    now[16] near the fire they nurse their wounds,
        warming now one now the other.

17   Their strength they trusted, and strove to be
        more mighty than all the others;
    their deserts, however, seemed to God
        to merit a different mead.

18   A life of lust they lived, many-wise,
        and of gold and jewels had joy:
    their reward now have they as walk they must
        between the frost and the fire.[17]

* * *

19   In sworn foes put thy faith never,
        though they woo thee with winsome words;
    speak fair to them, but others' fate
        'tis well to take as a warning.[18]

20 Found it Sorli so, the simple-hearted,[19]
      when he left the award[20] to Vígolf;
   he blindly trusted his brother's banesman,[21]
      who soon betrayed his trust.

21 Grith he gave them,[22] good-heartedly,
      and they pledged them to give him gold;
   all seemed well agreed while together they sate;
      yet soon was seen how they lied.

22 On the following day befell it then:
      when riding to Rýgiar-dale,
   they did to death who had done them naught,
      and left his body lifeless,

23 his hacked corse hauled by hidden path,
      and dropped it down a well:
   from the light would hide it; but the Lord did see,
      the holy one, from his heaven.

24 The true God then bade the good one's soul
      to enter into his bliss;
   but his evil foes will not early be
      relieved from e'erlasting pain.

* * *

25 Pray the "disar,"[23] the dear Lord's friends,
        be gracious and grant thee their favor:
    a week after will everything
        go as well as thou couldst wish.

26 What rashly thou wrought'st in anger—
        do not add more ill to it,
    but with good deeds soothe who was grieved by you;
        that, say they, is good for the soul.

27 To God shalt ever for good things pray,—
        to him who hath made all men;
    woefully ill fares every one
        who does not find his father.

28 Above all, beg that boon of him
        of which thou know'st most need;
    he misses all who asks for naught:
        heeds no one the silent one's needs.

29 Tardily came I, though called early,
        to the threshold of the throne.
    Thither will I, for that was the pledge:
        gets the prize[24] who pleadeth most.

30   Our sins cause it that with sorrow we fare
         out of this world of woe;
     need no one dread[25] who did no ill:
         't is well to be without blemish.

31   Like unto wolves I ween they be
         who have a fickle heart;[26]
     will they find it thus whose feet will have
         to fare on fiery paths.

32   Friendly redes shrewd, tied in a sheaf,
         sage counsels seven[27] I teach thee;
     heed thou give them, nor forget them ever:
         in good stead will they stand thee.

       * * *

33[28] It behooves me tell how happy I was
         and prized this world of pleasure;[29]
     and this also, how the sons of men
         dread to die from this world.

34   Pride and lust overpower those men
         who wish for worldly goods:
     the shining gold brings grief e'erlasting—
         hath wealth mocked full many.

Old Norse Poems

35   Aye fond of much men found me here,
         for little had I learned:[30]
     this life below[31] the Lord hath made
         full of lust and feasting.

36   Full long I sate, in sickness drooping—
         much then me listed to live;
     but he[32] prevailed who had more power:
         was I doomed to suffer death.

37   The ropes of hell[33] held me fast,
         when slung about my sides;
     tear them would I, but tough they were;
         unbound, one freely fares.

38   I alone knew in all ways how
         sorrows were heaped on my head:
     a world of horror those maids of hell
         did show me every eve.[34]

39   The sun I saw, the day-star in sooth,
         droop in the world of din;[35]
     but Hel's gate[36] heard I on the other hand
         grate with grinding.

40 The sun I saw, setting blood-red,
        when ready to wend from this world;
    mighty he seemed in many ways—
        far more than before.

41 The sun I saw: it seemed to me
        as on God Almighty I gazed;
    lowly before him[37] the last time I bowed,
        in this world of living wights.

42 The sun I saw, and so he shone
        that bereft of my senses I seemed;
    but over against him Gylfi's stream[38] roared
        in its bed, all mixed with blood.[39]

43 The sun I saw with trembling sight,
        affrighted and faint I was;
    for most woefully was my heart
        rent and torn in twain.[40]

44 The sun I saw, sadder never,
        when ready to wend from this world;
    like to wood my tongue did feel;
        grew my corpse all cold without.

45 The sun I saw, and since never,
        after that dreary day;
    far away the waters vanished:[41]
        cold, I parted from care.

46 From my breast did fly,— then born I was—
        and hence, my star of hope:[42]
    high it hovered, hastening on,
        never ceased it to soar.

47 Longer than any lasted that night[43]
        when, stiff, I lay on the straw;
    which soothly shows, as saith our Lord,
        that man is made of the mould.[44]

48 Knoweth, alas! the loving God,
        He who made heaven and earth,
    unloved how many must leave this world,
        though kith and kin they had.[45]

49 Of his works, every one the reward reapeth:
        happy he who does good:
    away from wealth, was I given
        a grave, dug in the gravel.[46]

50 The lust of the flesh oft lures on men—
        have many too much of that;
    the water of cleansing[47] was to me
        aye the most hateful of all.

51 On the norns' settle[48] sate I nine days;
        to the loftiest was I then lifted;
    out of clouded sky cruelly shone
        the sun that lights dead souls.[49]

52 Meseemed, through seven seats of victory[50]
        I fared, without and within;
    below and above I sought better ways,
        where most easily I could fare.

53 Now sooth I say of what first I saw
        as I passed to the world of pain:[51]
    with singed wings,[52] birds— souls they were—
        flew there as many as midges.

54 From the West saw I the Water-dragon[53] fly—
        he lighted on Lucifer's path;[54]
    his wings he shook so that far and wide
        were heaved up heaven and hell.

55 The Sun-stag[55] saw I, from the South faring—
        he tethered the two together;
    with his feet standing steadfast on earth,
        his horns touching very heaven.

56 From the North there came kinsmen[56] riding—
        seven saw I of them:
    out of full beakers pure beer they quaffed
        from out of Baugregin's burn.

57 The wind ceased, the water stopped;
        then heard I dreadful din:
    unfaithful wives for their wicked lovers
        ground there mould for meat.[57]

58 The dark women in dreary wise
        ground with the gory stones;[58]
    their bloody hearts, heavy with sorrow,
        about their breasts did hang.

59 Many a man maimed[59] I saw,
        walking the glowing ways.
    Methought their faces befouled all were
        with the gore of women beguiled.

60 Many a man to mould had grown
        who sacred supper[60] ne had;
    did heathen stars stand above them,
        blazing with baleful runes.

61 Men saw I there who much did feel
        envy of other men's lot:
    about their breasts were bloody runes
        marked with evil malice.

62 Men saw I there, many, cheerless,
        faring wilding ways:
    is rewarded thus in this world who
        fell a prey to follies.[61]

63 Men saw I there who in many ways
        had stolen what others owned;
    in flocks they fared to Fégiarn's[62] castle,
        laden with burdens of lead.[63]

64 Men saw I then who many a one
        had robbed of riches and life;
    poison-fanged snakes pierced these knaves,
        thrusting through their breasts.[64]

65 Men saw I then unmindful, in life,
        to hold dear the holy days:
    were their hands[65] now nailed on hot stones,
        as painful punishment.

66 Men saw I then of mighty pride,
        who held their heads too high:
    were their weeds all wondrously
        lined with living fire.

67 Men saw I then who many times
        had falsely lied on their fellows.
    Now Hell's ravens hacked felly
        their eyes out of their heads.

68 Thou canst not ever know all the pangs
        which the damned have in hell;
    their sweet sins turn to sore anguish:
        is pleasure e'er followed by pain.

69 Men saw I then, with merciful heart
        who had helped the humble;
    heavenly angels sang hymns above,
        and read holy books,[67] over their heads.

70 Men saw I then who had mortified
         with much fasting their flesh:
   the angels of God bowed to all of them,
         which is highest bliss in heaven.

71 Men saw I then who had meted out
         meat for the weary ones'[68] mouths:
   was their resting place on rays of heaven,
         forever at ease and in bliss.

72 Had holy maidens wholly cleansed and
         washed the souls of sin,
   of those men who on many days
         had scourged and scathed themselves.

73 Men saw I then in much who had
         heeded the laws of the Lord;
   were clean candles kindled over them
         which shone, burning brightly.

74 Saw I high wains fare the heavens along[69]—
         their ways led to the Lord;
   those men steered them who were murdered,
         though sinless themselves.

75   Oh mighty Father, oh matchless Son,
         oh Holy Ghost of Heaven:
     hearken to our prayer who hast made us,
         to free us all from evil!

76[70] Hringvor and Listvor sit at Herthi's[71] door,
         singing their siren strains:
     the Norn's blood from their noses drips,
         which whetteth hate among men.

77   Óthin's wife[72] on earth's ship[73] rows,
         lusting after love;
     'twill be late, ere that she lowers her sails,
         which are fastened by fleshly lusts.

78   Of thy heirloom, father, had I the care—
         I and Sólkatla's sons;[74]
     of the horn of that hart out of howe which bore
         wise Vígdvalin.

79   Here are runes which written have
         the nine daughters of Niorth:[75]
     Baugveig[76] the eldest, Kreppvor the youngest,
         and their seven sisters.

80 Every mortal sin committed they,
        Sváfr and Sváfrlogi;
    made well out the blood and sucked the wounds—
        ever ill in their ways.[77]

81 The lay which now learned thou[78] hast
        thou shalt speak and spread 'mongst the
    quick:
    the Sun Song, which in sooth will be
        found to be lying least.

82 Now must we part, but shall meet again
        when we rise again in gladness;[79]
    may our dear Lord grant their rest to the dead,[80]
        and eke his love to the living.

Old Norse Poems

Footnotes

1 With frequently only three syllables in the half-lines.

2 Also, with the Eddic poem *Fiolsvinnsmól*.

3 These have, somewhat unconvincingly, been compared to the Rune Poem of *Hóvamól* (139 f.); as, with better reason, the first portion to the "Óthin Ensamples" (*ibid.*, 91-100), and the second, to *Loddfáfnismól* (*ibid.*, 111-137).

4 This unnamed person is to be imagined as one of the bold solitary robbers who infested the forest and mountain fastnesses of Scandinavia.

5 Conjectural.

6 *I.e.*, the famished wayfarer. In the following, the personal pronoun applies, now to the one, now to the other.

7 Following B. M. Olsen's interpretation. The meaning seems to be that the grim outlaw, for once, takes pity on the frightened wayfarer; who afterwards ill requites him.

8 *I.e.*, overwelled.

9 At the moment. The stanza reminds one of the many platitudes of *Hugsvinnsmól* (see the Introduction): "man proposes, God disposes."

10 These names, as well as most others occurring in the poem, are evidently made to order.

11 The passage is not certain.

12 *I.e.*, as outlaws.

13 The first woman—or else, Adam and Eve—came sinless out of the hands of the Creator.

14 Duels were fought out on islands (holms); hence the expression "to go on the holm" for "to fight a duel."

15 Evidently a married couple, since Ráthný is a woman's name.

16 *I.e.*, in hell.

17 The damned are tortured both by heat and cold.

18 This very worldly, and certainly un-Christian, advice corresponds to *Hóvamól*, 89 f.

19 The term in the original may mean either one who gives good counsel or one who is easily deceived.

20 In certain cases, northern law allowed the award to be made by the fair-mindedness of one of the parties to a suit.

21 Cf. the warning *Sigrdrífumól*, 37.

22 The security is given by Sorli to his enemies.

23 Here, it seems, the *chorus virginum* that bear up the prayers of men to God. The following, rather prosy, stanzas are an elaboration on the theme of "pray and ye shall be given," somewhat in the form of the arch-heathen *Loddfáfnismál* (*Hóvamól*, 134 ff.), especially 32.

24 The crown of life.

25 Viz., the Judgment.

26 *I.e.*, are unsteady in the faith. To the medieval Christian, "doubt" is a mortal sin.

27 These counsels concerning the Deadly Sins—Pride, Covetousness, Lust, Anger, Gluttony, Envy, Sloth—seem to refer, in a loose fashion, rather to the preceding stanzas.

28 The following passage is the kernel of the poem. It deals with life and death, and life in the Beyond.

29 It is one of pleasure for those living, but one of terror for those suffering for their sins in hell.

30 That is, of what was to come.

31 Literally, this place for dwelling in (for a short while).

32 Satan?

33 *I.e.*, death.

34 The meaning of the stanza is doubtful. Possibly, the maids of hell are the diseases sent by Satan to torment the dying man.

35 It seems that this world below is meant, with its tumult and confusion, which reaches the speaker's ear as he lies on his deathbed, between this life and the Beyond.

36 The entrance to the realm of the dead, not necessarily the gates of the Christian hell; cf. the *Short Lay of Sigurth,* stanza 67.

37 *I.e.*, the sun, which is feminine in Old Norse. According to Ólson, this passage shows that the sun is not here to be taken as a symbol (of Christ), but physically.

38 Kenning for "the sea." (?).

39 *I.e.*, reflecting the bloody red of sunset.

40 Viz., by contrition, knowing that his last hour has struck.

41 Accepting Ólsen's interpretation: As the eyes of the dying man close, both sun and sea vanish to him.

42 The "star of hope" has been interpreted as the soul, departing from the body at the time of birth, viz., into another life: there is an intimate connection between each human life and its "star."

43 The night of the "wake."

44 Cf. *Genesis* 3:19, "Dust thou art," etc.

45 The poet seems to complain that the nearest of kin often do not show loving care for the dying.

46 Separated from his wealth by death, every man's destiny is the same.

47 That is, from sin.

48 According to Ólson, whose text I follow here, this is the Hill of Purgatory (cf. Dante's Mountain of Purgatory) where the soul dwells nine days, to be cleansed from nine deadly sins, then to be lifted up to the highest pinnacle.

49 A difficult passage, but there is no doubt reference to the light of another world.

50 In this obscure stanza, the "seats of victory" seem to signify the stations on the way from Hell to Paradise. According to medieval tradition there are seven worlds obedient to Christ.

51 *I.e.,* hell.

52 Because coming out of the fire of cleansing.

53 Leviathan?

54 The glowing Pool (?). The stanza as a whole is obscure.

55 Very likely, Christ, who in such legends as those of Placitus, Hubertus, etc., appears as a stag with the cross between his antlers. He comes to bind together Leviathan and Lucifer (?).

56 According to Ólson, the seven Wise Men of the old dispensation, who (like Dante's poets and sages of antiquity) are placed at the very entrance, in a *limbus patrum,* where they indulge in their earthly habits not subjected to torture. But, more convincingly, Paasche points out that in the homilies, *baugr,* "ring," signifies God's mercy. Hence the-burn-of-the-god(*regin*)-of-the-ring is a kenning for Christ, who is the "fountain of mercy" (*fons misericordiæ*) which refreshes the angels.

57 Evidently, as punishment for adultery. The following stanzas refer to the punishment of the wicked and the reward of the pious.

58 *I.e.,* millstones.

59 Emasculated? The stanza evidently refers to the punishment of lecherers.

60 Holy Communion. It is, doubtfully, suggested that, without it, man is threatened by signs foreboding hell-torment.

61 The stanza seems to refer to the punishment of Vanity.

62 "Greedy for Money," *i.e.*. Mammon.

63 Instead of the gold they had craved.

64 As they had run others through with their swords.

65 The Sabbath-breakers are punished in the member by which they offended.

66 The sin of Pride was exhibited chiefly ir their garments.

67 The "Book of Life," probably, in which the names of the blessed are recorded. In the following stanzas the reward of the "virtuous" is pictured.

68 Meant are the pilgrims.

69 Scholars have suggested that the poet was thinking of the wain of Elijah.

70 In the following, exceedingly difficult stanzas, the poet seems to return to the punishment of the wicked. So emended by Ólsen; if correctly, *Hringvor* refers to the sin of Slander, as *Listvor* does to Treason. both personified as women in the guise of sirens. Their emanations spread strife among men.

71 As Ólsen ingeniously suggests, possibly corrupted from (H)*Erebi*, genitive of *Erebus*, the lower world.

72 Apparently, here *Venus* (*Freya*).

73 The earth viewed as a ship (?). Or can the poet here possibly refer to Venus in her shell drifting on the main?

74 Paasche suggests that *Sólkatla* is the Heavenly Jerusalem; her sons, therefore, the company of Saints. But none of the conjectures so far offered seem to clear up this obscure stanza, whose translation, therefore, mildly put, is uncertain.

75 Hardly the god *Niorth*.

76 Possibly, this name refers to the sin of Avarice, "the oldest of the sins," as *Kreppvor* to Pride. Their sisters are the other mortal sins.

77 It has been suggested that the meaning is: once men surrender to the deadly sins they become "wolves," *i.e.*, commit even unnatural sins.

78 Viz., the son, from his departed father.

79 *Dies Lætitiæ*.

80 The *Requiem æternum dona eis* of Catholic prayer.

Lee M. Hollander

Abela Publishing

republishing

YESTERDAY'S BOOKS

for

TOMORROW'S EDUCATIONS

www.AbelaPublishing.com